c1

73032

B
KEFAU- Swados, Harvey
VER   Standing up for the
         people

Date Due

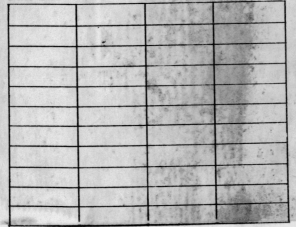

Biography of Estes Kefauver, U.S. Senator from Kentucky and perennial presidential aspirant, who earned many enemies primarily because of the way he used his office to investigate the cost to the people of corruption and monopoly.

STANDING UP
FOR THE PEOPLE

STANDING UP
FOR THE PEOPLE

THE LIFE AND WORK OF
ESTES KEFAUVER

HARVEY SWADOS

E. P. DUTTON & CO., INC.   NEW YORK

We gratefully acknowledge permission to reprint from
In a Few Hands, by Estes Kefauver, copyright © 1965 by
Nancy P. Kefauver; reprinted by permission of Pantheon
Books, a division of Random House, Inc., and *The Great
Price Conspiracy,* by John Herling, copyright © 1962 by
John Herling; reprinted by permission of Robert B. Luce,
Inc.

Published simultaneously in Canada by Clarke,
Irwin & Company Limited, Toronto and Vancouver

SBN: 0–525–39872–4 LCC: 79–179055

Designed by Hilda Scott
Printed in the U.S.A.
First Edition

For Robin—
and all the other young Americans
who will be voting at 18

ACKNOWLEDGMENTS

The writing of this book has been a political act. I owe the pressure to carry it through to my friend, the poet and editor Peter Hyun; and the essential collaboration and research support to my wife, Bette Swados.

Among those who have helped contribute to my education I am happy to acknowledge with gratitude the children of Estes and Nancy Kefauver, most particularly, Lynda; and the following hospitable and patient people in these places visited:

In New York: Boris Kostelanetz, the late Elmo Roper, Samuel Ungerleider.

In Washington, D.C.: Dr. John Blair, Mr. and Mrs. Richard Borwick, Charles Caldwell, Senator Paul Douglas, Benjamin Gordon, Lucile Myers, Jowanda Shelton, Clarence K. Streit, Charles Tyroler II, Richard Wallace.

In Madisonville: Nora Kefauver.

In Knoxville: John Dobson, Curator of the indispensable Estes Kefauver Collection at the University of Tennessee Library, Mrs. Nancy Kefauver Fooshee.

In Chattanooga: Harry Mansfield, Jack Reddy.

In Nashville: Mrs. Tom Ragland.

In Memphis: the Honorable Edmund Orgill, former Mayor of Memphis, and all those foregathered with him one day at the Tennessee Club to reminisce about Estes Kefauver.

Amherst, Mass.
January 1971

HARVEY SWADOS

☆ Contents

Photos appear between pages 96 and 97.

a foreword ☆ Who He Was and What He Wanted

☆☆☆ This is the story of one of the most misunderstood men of modern times. Mention the name of Estes Kefauver to anyone outside Tennessee who remembers him as a public figure: More than likely he will be recalled as the Senator who ran the sensational crime investigation that became one of the early TV hit shows, or as the perennial candidate who was so eager to be President that he made a fool of himself, clapping a coonskin cap on his head in order to amuse the yokels, and shaking so many hands that he would even reach for his wife's.

Such misconceptions are cruel and unjust both to him and to ourselves: To him because they allow the distortions of his rivals and his enemies to pass, unchallenged, as the verdict of history; to ourselves because they deprive us of the inspiration of a man of rare quality, whose twenty-five years of public life were spent not in strutting in the limelight, nor in enriching himself, but in fighting for causes that are far more significant to us today than they were in Estes Kefauver's time.

His time, in fact, is now. Merely to enumerate the causes he espoused (and fought for at the cost of making im-

placable enemies) is to begin to understand both his histori-
cal importance and his contemporary relevance for the new
generation. At home, he fought against crimes committed
not just by the underworld but by the captains of industry.
His painstaking exposures of the greed and folly of the steel
industry, the auto industry, the communications industry,
the baking business, and above all the drug manufacturers,
made him a man uniquely trusted by millions, with countless admirers among the poor and the powerless.

His battle to protect and defend the Tennessee Valley
Authority against the utility combines foreshadowed our
current concern with the defense of our environment against
its despoilers. His firm refusal to join his fellow Southern
Senators in defying the United States Supreme Court's ban
on segregated schools gained him a rare respect and affection among Negroes. His opposition to the anti-Communist
hysteria not just of the McCarthyites but of such 1950's
liberals as Hubert Humphrey would place him today in the
forefront of those concerned with civil rights as a moral and
not simply a vote-getting issue.

Estes Kefauver was undeterred by the fact that his stand
on these issues brought him into conflict with the attitudes
of many in his home state on whom he depended for re-
election to the Senate—to say nothing of the rich and powerful in the country at large. Had he been deterred, he would
never have supported (as he did, unflinchingly, for the
better part of twenty years) the concept of Atlantic Union,
of a federated government of the democracies of the Western world. For his pains, this brilliant and thoughtful man
was reviled in Tennessee as a "nigger-loving one-worlder,"
and in the country at large was cartooned as a small-town
bumpkin with ambitions too big for his little mind.

Because of the way in which he made use of his office—
primarily the careful investigation of the cost to the people
of corruption and monopoly—he earned many enemies,
particularly among the professional politicians who stood
between him and the Presidency to which he had aspired.
But his patent sincerity, courage, and unparalleled skill in
clarifying complex economic and political problems for
the common man made plain people regard him as a model
of what a public servant ought to be.

"It is in the third branch of government, the legislative
branch," former Senator Joseph Clark has written in *The
Senate Establishment,* "where political lag remains trium-
phant, and where the twentieth-century men are not in
charge. Though the Senate has been shaken by wars, deaths,
the electorate, and other calamities, those in it dedicated to
the preservation of the status quo in economic and property
rights and to the past in human rights—that bipartisan conservative coalition which I have called the 'Senate establishment'—have still not given way to the new generation."

Estes Kefauver was one of those who spoke for that new
generation. If he were alive, he would speak for it today—
not because he appointed himself as anyone's spokesman,
but simply because he was one of the lonely soldiers of the
common good, as Paul Douglas has characterized the small
band of twentieth-century men in Congress. As such he
articulated, throughout his decade and a half in the Senate,
the best aspirations of young people for a more humane
and just society, freed from the shackles of fraud and greed.

From the outset Estes Kefauver understood and grasped
what Donald R. Matthews, in *U.S. Senators and Their
World,* has described as the Senate's "unequaled opportunity to educate and lead the people." In consequence, his

reputation, as Joseph Clark has said in *Congress: The Sapless Branch,* "will long survive in history."

But it was this very determination to educate and to lead —his ambition, his detractors called it—that brought Estes Kefauver into collision with the Senate establishment and later with the executive, and stymied him in his own efforts to reach the White House. It made little difference to them that plaudits for his industry and integrity came from the labor movement, the civil rights organizations, even from the Junior Chamber of Commerce; that early in his Senatorial career *Time* magazine named him as one of the Senate's ten most valuable members; or that before his first term had expired he was voted by the Washington press corps second only to Paul Douglas as the nation's best Senator. For in his determination to lead, as well as in his standing up for the people, for principles that went beyond sectionalism, he violated the unwritten rules of both the professional politicians and the Senate establishment. Inevitably, he won the bitter, undying opposition of those without whose neutrality—if not support—he could not hope to make it to the top.

To appreciate both the irony and the drama in this conflict, we shall have to begin at the beginning.

STANDING UP
FOR THE PEOPLE

one ☆ Early Days

☆☆☆ As the twentieth century was getting under way, two boys were born to the Kefauvers of Madisonville, Tennessee, a small town midway between Chattanooga and Knoxville. Robert arrived in 1901 and his younger brother, Carey Estes, was born on July 26, 1903. The brothers were joined later by two sisters, Nancy and Nora, and all grew up together in a large frame house on the outskirts of town. Grandfather Kefauver had been a Baptist pastor given to two-hour sermons, first in Chattanooga, then in Madisonville. His son Robert Cooke Kefauver did well in the hardware and farm-implement business, invested in local real estate, settled down to farming, and served five terms as Madisonville's unpaid mayor. He married into the old colonial Estes family—Phredonia Estes Kefauver was a niece of Judge Joe Estes of Memphis and a cousin of Governor Joe Folk, who gained fame by fighting corruption in Missouri.

Robert and Estes were happy country boys who enjoyed bicycling and playing together in the woods, with Robert almost always the leader and Estes the tag-along kid brother. Even in his earliest childhood, Estes impressed people as being serious and thoughtful. When he was four years old, he watched his Aunt Charlotte's dog bark vociferously at every leap while chasing a rabbit across a field. "If Laddie would quit barking so much and save his breath," Estes remarked, shaking his head, "he could run faster and catch the rabbit."

Robert was the brighter and quicker of the two boys, adored not only by his younger brother but by the rest of the family as well. Robert was the more aggressive of the two, according to their sister, Nancy Kefauver Fooshee, who used to debate with herself: Which do I love better? "My uncle had to wash Robert's mouth out with tar soap once, and when my younger sister was born he said to mother, 'Huh, I'd rather have a billy goat.' " It came as a terrible tragedy when, during the summer of Estes' eleventh year, Robert was stricken while swimming in the Tellico River with the local crowd. Estes was the best swimmer of the lot, and, when Robert went under, the farthest away. Thrashing back across the river, he tried desperately to revive his brother and then, with the aid of his friends, carried him home. Robert lingered on for some days, unconscious, but at length went into convulsions and died.

The death of his admired older brother left Estes shaken and brooding. For months on end he kept to his room, left by his mourning parents to read, hour after hour, the biographies and histories that were to serve as the foundation of his later education. When at last he ended his mourning, he emerged with a new determination and a new ambition: "I felt," he said, "that I had to do better to make up to my parents for his loss."

From that time on, Estes rarely spoke of his brother. We have no way of knowing how large a part the tragic incident played in the development of the growing young man's character. Yet, nearly half a century later, only a few days before his own death, Estes talked of his long-dead brother to a devoted member of his staff, Jowanda Shelton. "If there is anything to religion," he said to her, "I ought to see my brother Robert again. I suppose it's odd, but I wonder to myself, if we'd meet, would he be a grown man?"

A tall, gangling lad, Estes went along with his father in the summer of 1916, nailing campaign posters to the trees for President Woodrow Wilson. HE KEPT US OUT OF WAR, the Democratic posters proclaimed to Republican Monroe County—they were Estes' introduction to the world of politics. The following year, his mother took him along for a trip to Washington, where he met her cousin Joe Folk, the former Governor of Missouri.

"What do you want to be when you grow up, son?" Folk asked him.

Estes did not hesitate. "A lawyer," he announced, confirming the ambition he had already confided in his father a good ten years earlier.

He was a teenager when he discovered how much excitement there was inside the old red-brick courthouse in the heart of town. One day he drifted in off the tree-lined streets and was at once caught up in the drama of a case in progress. The conflict of ideas, the beauty of logic, and the fire of eloquence stirred him while he watched the virtuoso performances of his favorites—Judge Sam Epps Young of Sweetwater, Eugene Irvings of Athens, Judge Matt Whitaker of Chattanooga.

He got on the high school debating team, he conducted mock trials, and he kept a scrapbook in which he pasted speeches of political candidates and news stories about government. Later on, he couldn't remember much of the issues that were debated in the courthouse where he had sat eagerly drinking it all in, except that one interminable

case involved three feuding families, and that every time
there was a trial someone else got shot. What mattered was
that he had caught fire, and was unshakable in his determination to become a lawyer.

During his high school years his ambitions sometimes
soared even higher. When a school friend gave him her
friendship book to sign he wrote, under his signature:
AMBITION—To be President.

He gave no indication, though, that he had it in him to be
anything other than what he was—a big strapping fellow
who did only moderately well in school and was considered,
although he was quite popular, to be a pretty ordinary boy.
What impressed his family, friends, and teachers far more
than his intellect or his grades was the gentleness of his disposition and a modesty that was actually humility. It is a remarkable testimony, when you consider it, that it is impossible to find a single relative or friend who can recall Estes
ever displaying anger. This calmness and affability made it
possible for him to assume positions of leadership even in his
high school days without arousing feelings of resentment
and stood him in good stead through the greater trials of
public life.

His long-time secretary, Lucile Myers, believes that his
gentle consideration was one of the prime causes for the
fanatic loyalty of his staff and their willingness to put in
fantastically long hours. "In all of those years," she says, "I
can remember his being short with me just once. I was trying
to hang on to his attention for some matter, and he finally
said to me in exasperation, 'Listen, you're going to make
me miss my plane.' And do you know, when he got to the
airport he called the office and apologized to me?"

During his high school days, Estes spent summer vaca-

tions working at his Uncle Joe Estes' farm in Orysa, in West
Tennessee, where he cut hay, hunted eggs, sawed wood,
milked cows, and plowed. A six-footer by now, he could
take a two-bushel sack of wheat by the sewed-up top in one
hand, and hold it at arm's length. Like his ability to push
the cap off a Coke bottle with the thumb of one hand, it was
not the sort of thing that people easily forgot. As he filled
out and lost his gawkiness, he went in for sports, playing
center on the Madisonville High basketball team and center
field on its baseball team. Still reserved and quiet, he did
become secretary-treasurer of his senior class and editor of
the yearbook.

Even though his grades were not outstanding, Estes had
reason to feel confident that he would do well at the University of Tennessee, and that he would be respected by his
classmates. He had no way of knowing that, even on a cam-
pus which in 1920 was hardly a center of elegance and cos-
mopolitanism, he would be regarded as a hopeless hick, a
dumb yokel. Gaping at him as he scrambled off the train in
Knoxville, his cousin Thomas Walker was so embarrassed
by his appearance that he took him into his fraternity house,
Kappa Sigma, by way of the side door.

Writing of this humiliation years later, Estes Kefauver
recalled how he had prepared to take the town by storm.
He wore a new iridescent suit from a mail-order catalogue,
a small cap, two stickpins, and his Sunday school buttons.
It was no wonder that one of the fraternity brothers, staring
at Estes' chest, adorned with the two rows of awards for per-
fect Sunday school attendance, whispered to Thomas
Walker, "Where did you find that rube?"

Stung by this reception, by the constant heckling demand, "Where did you get that hat?" and by the poor im-

pression he made on Coach Bender when he went out for
football (there hadn't been a football team at Madisonville), Estes returned home dejected and humiliated after
his first weeks in Knoxville, his dreams of being a successful
and popular college man fading before his eyes.

His mother saw at once that he was miserable, and took
him to her bedroom for a long talk. Then she gave him what
he was to call "the best advice I ever received."

She urged him to turn his stumbling blocks into stepping-stones, and to use his disappointment as a spur to study
more.

This kind of talk will no doubt strike the modern reader
as corny or square. But it should serve to remind us that like
all of the most aware people of his generation, Estes
Kefauver spanned two eras as distinct technologically as they
were ethically. Deeply involved in the 1960's in the struggle
for public control of applied science and communications,
Kefauver the Senator had to acquire expertise in such super-
modern technologies as antibiotics, space technology, satellite transmissions; yet his own father had brought to Madisonville the first automobile ever seen in Monroe County
(there were a total of six automobiles in Knoxville at the
time), and indeed owned the first bicycle ever brought into
Monroe County.

If we bear this in mind, we may find it more understand-
able that Estes' mother Phredonia (of a family noted in
Renaissance Italy, taking its name from Villa d'Este, the
family seat in Tivoli) wrote him every day during his
undergraduate college years. She instilled in him the moral
righteousness that served later as a kind of ethical base for
his own brand of Populism. "Leave no tender word unsaid,"
she wrote him. And, on another occasion: "Do good while
life shall last."

For Estes these were not joking matters, but admonitions to be accepted and acted upon. After the weekend with his mother, he went back to school determined to make stepping-stones of stumbling blocks.

After football practice each day he worked an extra half hour, hitting the dummy in an effort to convert his weak blocking and tackling into a strength. His game improved so that he made the varsity and found himself a popular boy at the Kappa Sigma house.

"I paid for my room by stoking the furnace. Getting up early on cold winter mornings, I felt sorry for myself. Once awake, I couldn't go back to sleep. But two hours' study while the other fellows slept and my mind was fresh gave me the extra push I needed in classwork. Before the four years were over I had turned enough stumbling blocks into stepping-stones to receive my share of honors in scholastics and sports."

He had a certain reason for pride. He had not only made the football team, but also the track team (of which he became captain); he became editor of the student newspaper and president of the junior class and, in his senior year, president of the Southern Federation of College Students.

Six feet three by now, a rather imposing young man, Estes Kefauver's rather solemn face was that of a would-be lawyer —but it would be a mistake to think of him as either stuffy or self-satisfied, then or later. Elmo Roper, the public opinion analyst, recalled the day when Justice Owen Roberts of the Supreme Court said to Senator Kefauver, "I do wish you'd clear up for me the question of whether or not you were once an All-American football player."

"When I first ran for Congress," Kefauver replied gravely, "the newspapers identified me simply as a college football player. When I ran for re-election I was referred to as a star football player. When I ran for the Senate I had become Old Ironsides, an athletic hero. And when I ran for the Vice Presidency I was called an All-American football player." Without cracking a smile he added, "The truth of the matter is that I was a substitute."

Estes was anxious to go on to law school, but his mother fell ill and he drove her and his sister Nancy to Hot Springs, Arkansas, for a prolonged rest. In the fall he got a job teaching math and serving as athletic coach at Hot Springs High School. "Estes would have killed himself," his sister Nancy recalls, "in order to get things for me and my sister. In Hot Springs he'd take me as his date to a dance hall, just so I could have someone to go out with and have a good time."

At the end of the year he was offered twenty-five hundred dollars to stay on at Hot Springs High. It was a terrific salary for someone his age, but his mother was getting better, and Estes still knew what he really wanted. Within a day he had made the decision, and he announced to his father, "I want to go to Yale to study law."

His father was more than pleased. He gave Estes a hundred dollars to speed him on his way. But the speed was a little less than father or son had counted on—Estes and his buddy Jack Doughty went into partnership to buy an old Model-T Ford, which died on them in Virginia, and they had to hitchhike somewhat ingloriously on up to New Haven.

Estes' arrival in New Haven may have been a bit less starry-eyed than his appearance in Knoxville with his flashy mail-order suit, but by now he was both more realistic and more mature. He worked hard in law school, where he was somewhat overshadowed academically by such classmates as Robert M. Hutchins, Herbert Brownell, Jr., and Brien

McMahon, later U.S. Senator from Connecticut—whom he solemnly assured, as they shook hands in farewell, "I'll see you in Washington." He worked hard too in the jobs he took to support himself. He began by firing furnaces and washing dishes, but when his father objected that this would inter- fere with his legal studies, Estes tutored well-to-do students, in addition to clerking in a bookstore and waiting on tables. In the summer he sold Bibles all over East Tennessee. He accepted very little money from his father, but he did create something of a sensation when he turned up in Madison- ville during Christmas vacation in a coonskin overcoat given him by one of his affluent—and grateful—students.

In 1927 he was graduated from Yale Law School with honors. He was twenty-four years old, and ready to step out into the world.

two ☆ Starting Out

☆☆☆ The logical thing, Estes thought, would be to start big—go to Washington and enter the international law firm of ex-Governor Joe Folk, the distinguished cousin whom he had visited as a teenager. But the death of Folk destroyed this dream, and after shopping around fruitlessly in Knoxville, Estes got desk space in the library of a Chattanooga firm dominated by some other kinfolk—Cooke, Swaney, and Cooke—in return for running errands. There he sat anxiously for two weeks before his first client, a grocer trying to collect seventeen dollars, came in.

During his first two years of practice, he handled the most humble kinds of legal problems by day and taught at the Chattanooga College of Law by night. It was not exactly lucrative: After a year of defending men charged with stealing trousers, young women seeking divorces, and old women searching for help, he found that he had earned exactly eight hundred dollars.

But if he was not getting rich he was learning a lot about the poor who are supposedly protected by the law, but are all too often its victims. It was not exactly by chance that most of his clients were Negroes, since they could afford no one more prestigious than a struggling young lawyer—and were glad to have him represent them when they saw how he fought for their rights. An old charwoman, grateful when he won a case for her and then showed her how to bank the money, brought the lawyer one troubled client after another. To Kefauver these people deserved the best that was in him not just because they were black, but more importantly because they were poor and therefore not only unaware of their rights but unsure of how to go about gaining them.

All the while, though, he was managing to have a pretty good time. If there wasn't enough money to get through the week, there were friends from whom he was constantly bumming cigarettes and toothpaste, like his fellow bachelor, Jack Reddy, later to become a U.S. Attorney and a prominent Chattanooga lawyer. For a year or so the two roomed and ate together in the home of the folks of a Chattanooga Congressman. Then, as later, Estes liked a good game of bridge, a good bottle of scotch, and good-looking girls; he was as personally warm with Reddy and their friends, and as unable to generate bitterness, as he had been at home with his own family.

A Negro servant named Percy was employed by the young boarders to keep house. Every morning at the breakfast table he would greet them with, "What'll you have this morning?" No matter how they answered, he would serve scrambled eggs and coffee. They got used to the monotonous diet, but when they discovered that Percy was dipping into their precious grog, they decided that he would have to go, and drew straws to see who would tell him. Estes lost.

Despite the repeated urgings of his friends, he kept putting off the unpleasant task. Finally, one morning, after Reddy and Kefauver had divided the morning paper between them, Percy came in with his usual demand: "What'll it be?" Without looking up, his face buried in the paper, Kefauver blurted out, "Percy, you're fired!" And his relief, when Percy took the news as something he had been expecting, was simply enormous. It was just about the last time he would be able to bring himself to fire anybody.

"The lawyer whom I most admired," Kefauver reflected in later years, "was Mr. J. B. Sizer, who had started his practice in Madisonville and then built up a large firm in Chattanooga. My ambition was to become one of his legal helpers with a chance of eventually working my way into a partnership. He had nothing for me, but said he would keep me in mind."

In December 1927 the *Tennessee Law Review* published a substantial piece Kefauver had written on the development of the law on corporation practices. It attracted the attention of the firm of Sizer, Chambliss, and Sizer, and Kefauver began to feel that maybe things were looking up. But then a widow came to him for help in obtaining compensation from a railroad company for her husband's accidental death.

When I wrote to the company [Kefauver recalled] I found to my dismay that their legal representative was Mr. Sizer's firm. The tone of the reply, from Mr. Sizer himself, showed that he felt strongly that ours was not a legitimate case. It seemed clear that if I went ahead with it I could forget about working for him. But I had gone too far to retreat honorably.

A few days later I was in the courtroom, face to face with Mr. Sizer. I was terribly embarrassed, but I had worked hard on preparing my client's case and I presented it to the best of my ability. Mr. Sizer hardly looked at me during the proceedings, and when the judge announced the verdict in my favor he left without a word.

Next morning I was called to Mr. Sizer's office. To my amazement he said, "Estes, I liked the way you handled that case." Before I left his office he had arranged for me to become not merely a salaried employee but a junior partner. I had never turned a bigger stumbling block into a finer stepping-stone.

Indeed he had not. In March 1930 the firm of Sizer, Chambliss, and Sizer became Sizer, Chambliss, and Kefauver.

Depression had struck America, and the young lawyer concentrated on building his practice. Colleagues like Jack Reddy think back on him as both a busy and a good civil lawyer, who rapidly became one of the top trial lawyers in town. Reddy adds, "He took on criminal cases too, which in those days was only good in helping the underdog."

Involved as he was in the intricacies of banking and finance (he had become counsel for several banks) and in Chattanooga and East Tennessee civic problems, Kefauver led a very active social life—in part, many think, because of his deep-seated fear of being alone. That fear—evidenced by his gravity, even somberness, and the feeling even among those closest to him that they didn't really *know* him—was never to leave him. Many years later, in the summer of 1952, he was campaigning in the Oregon primary, accompanied by an administrative assistant, Charlie Neese (now a judge). In order that Kefauver might get some rest before a scheduled speech, Neese saw to it that their arrival was unpublicized, and went off to a movie as soon as the Senator had fallen asleep. When he returned from the movie he was astonished to find Kefauver, in pajamas and bathrobe, entertaining a room packed with people. Unabashed, Kefauver explained, "Well, Charlie, there wasn't anybody here when I woke up—so I called up a few people I know."

Unquestionably the biggest thing that happened to Kefauver in that tumultuous depression decade was meeting Nancy Pigott in the summer of 1934. Nancy was a pretty redhead who had been raised in a town house in Glasgow, the daughter of Sir Stephen Pigott of New York and Mary Lewis of Chattanooga; her father, a naval engineer, had gone to Scotland a quarter of a century earlier and stayed on to become manager of a Clydebank shipping concern, knighted for his design of the turbine engines for the *Queen Mary* and the *Queen Elizabeth*. Nancy and her sister Eleanor were brought up so strictly that they were seventeen years old before they were allowed to eat at the same table with their parents.

Nancy had gone to Glasgow College of Art, where she was graduated second in her class, and then on to Paris, where she studied under the cubist, André Lhote. After a year in London working as a designer, decorator, and book illustrator, she and Eleanor sailed off on their first visit to America, to meet their mother's family in Chattanooga.

For Kefauver, this cultivated, green-eyed girl, whom he had met on a blind double-date, represented beauty and a kind of dashing elegance that spoke of a world far beyond not just Madisonville, but Chattanooga as well. After their American visit, the Pigott sisters returned to New York to sail for Glasgow and found the tall lawyer waiting at the ship to see them off. In the course of the year that followed he bombarded her with letters, and the following summer set sail with a handsome and suave friend, Corry Smith, determined to marry her.

At the pier they were met by the Pigotts. Before anyone could say anything, Mrs. Pigott had thrown her arms around Corry Smith, crying, "I always hoped my daughter would marry someone just like you!"

Kefauver was undeterred by the slight. In short order he married the girl he had come so far to claim, and they went off to Loch Ness on their honeymoon.

They had no sooner settled down back in Tennessee than Kefauver was once again deep in his law practice, and also in a number of activities that were to lay the basis for his entrance into politics.

three ☆ Getting into Politics

☆☆☆ Some of the people who knew him at the time feel that it was the issue of public versus private electrical power, and the protection and extension of public power, that first took Estes Kefauver into politics. Others, that his commitment was broader—to an activist politics practiced on behalf of the small people—farmers, workers, small businessmen, storekeepers—who had been struggling for half a century and more against the massive economic and political power of big business and monopolies.

Maybe it was something of both. After all, the Tennessee Valley Authority, the remarkable agency that altered the geography of Kefauver's home state and the lives of millions of rural Southerners, had been fathered by the great independent Senator, George W. Norris of Nebraska, as a means of bringing power and light into the lives of powerless and isolated Americans. Vetoed by both Presidents Coolidge and Hoover, it was finally endorsed by President Roosevelt as part of his New Deal program and brought into being over the bitter opposition of private power interests, who called it costly and socialistic.

By means of an independent corporate agency, the Federal government took over Wilson Dam and other installations and used them as the nucleus of a vast scheme of regional planning and integrated development of an area of some forty thousand square miles. Financed by Congressional appropriations, the sale of surplus power, and bond issues, TVA was also authorized to build more dams in order to generate hydroelectric power, control the floods that periodically ravaged the area, and improve navigation.

Not only did TVA bring electricity to millions of farm homes; it assisted farmers with conservation, promoted industrial expansion, and conducted surveys on social and economic conditions. In cooperation with local authorities —unlike other Federal agencies, TVA's headquarters were located not in Washington but in the region—TVA engaged in malaria control, tree-planting, and development of natural resources and recreational facilities on the banks of reservoirs. Its system of multipurpose dams that dominate the life of the valley has been so remarkably successful that they, and indeed the entire program, have become a model for similar river projects throughout the world.

During the Eisenhower administration, resurgent private interests made a determined effort to gut TVA, and evoked from an aroused Kefauver one of his most brilliant and swiftly executed responses in behalf of the ordinary Americans who had been benefiting from TVA and were unaware of what was being proposed.

But that is a story which must come later. In the thirties, the problem was one of attracting investors to a state which because of TVA was just emerging from the kerosene era, and of attacking the corruption which was as powerful a brake on its growth as the lack of electric power had been. Estes Kefauver, who had been gaining public attention with a series of page-one articles in the Chattanooga *News* on public power and local government reform, was invited to join a group called The Volunteers. (Every football fan knows that Tennessee, with its unusually high percentage of volunteers for the armed forces throughout American history, has become known as the Volunteer State.)

The Volunteers battled against the corruption of a local political machine which, in order to build up revenue, had helpless Negroes hauled into court practically by the truckload for minor offenses simply in order to collect fines from them. Kefauver decided that the best way for him to attack the problem would be to run for office, and in 1938 he ran for state senator, supported not only by the Chattanooga *News* and *Times,* but also by organized labor.

He lost. But in the course of losing, some interesting things happened, both to Kefauver and to the people of his district.

For one, when he rang the doorbell of the Mansfield family, asking for support, the door was opened by young Harry, who became an immediate convert. At an ice cream supper not long thereafter, twelve-year-old Harry tried to sell him some tickets; Kefauver (who was yearning for a son) asked him if he'd like to put that initiative to work in his campaign.

Harry got the okay from his mother and soon found himself trotting alongside the tall, earnest campaigner, passing out handbills and sitting on Kefauver's broad shoulders to put up posters, much as Estes himself had done for his own father in the Wilson campaign. To this day, Mansfield remembers: "He didn't like to carry money, so he'd give it to me to hold for him."

Small wonder that the boy worshiped the older man. Kefauver lost by a few hundred votes, and Harry wept in frustration. But their relationship was not to end there.

Years later, when Kefauver was established in Washington, he sent for Harry to come and work for him full-time. "When I went into the service," Mansfield says, "he kept in touch with me through the War Department," and many years later, after John Kennedy had become President, one of the two jobs that Senator Kefauver requested of him was that of U.S. Marshal for Harry Mansfield.

"I felt like as long as he was around I didn't have any problems," says Mansfield. "He was like a father to me."

The other noteworthy element of an otherwise unmemorable campaign was the big candidate's dogged fight against the entrenched political organizations. It made a profound impression upon the Nashville liberals, who decided that he was a man worth watching even though his dawn-to-dusk handshaking, combined with a memory that was faulty (to put it mildly), gave rise to stories that were to crop up again and again throughout his political career.

One, detailed by Jack Anderson and Fred Blumenthal in *The Kefauver Story,* was destined to become both legendary and typical of the candidate's mixture of simple charm and terrible absentmindedness. After a speech, he shook hands with an eager teenager, saying, "I'm Estes Kefauver."

"My name is Johnny Thomas."

"Glad to know you, Johnny. Who's your father?"

"My father's dead."

"Oh, I'm sorry."

That same night, Kefauver ran into a young man and offered him a handshake. "I'm Estes Kefauver," the candidate said.

"My name is Johnny Thomas."

"Nice meeting you, Johnny. And what does your father do?"

"He's still dead."

Within weeks, the defeated candidate for the state senate was approached by the victorious candidate for the governorship: Would he take on the job of finance and taxation commissioner? After a little persuasion, Kefauver said yes.

He stayed in Nashville only four months, but with almost spectacular results. He introduced simplified tax-collecting methods, which raised the state's income by cutting down on tax-dodging, and at the same time brought administrative costs down to one of the lowest figures in the country. Hardworking and knowledgeable, he quickly won the gratitude of the new Governor, who praised him as "one of the most valuable men in my cabinet."

Tax reform, when it truly attacks the privileged who benefit most from inequities, is extremely difficult to get through any legislature. Kefauver's reform bill just barely achieved passage, and he was free to return to his law practice in Chattanooga.

But not for long. Later that year, the Congressman who had been serving for sixteen years from Tennessee's third district died. Kefauver decided that his moment had come. Although he had the support of New Dealers and TVA enthusiasts—he ran on a program of Federal aid to education—a little closer to home the feeling was more tempered. His own father, to whom he always turned for advice, felt that Estes was jeopardizing a good law practice for something as risky as politics, and when he dropped in on Jack Reddy in Washington, his former roommate sat him down in a restaurant on 11th Street and tried to talk him out of making the race. "I said, 'Estes, Congressmen are a dime a dozen here in Washington.' But Estes had been bitten, and from then on he would never need much urging to run for office."

From then on he would never be beaten in Tennessee either. He expected a tough battle against the Hamilton County machine, but to his own surprise and that of many others the county boss, hoping to hang on by going with a potential winner, came out for Kefauver. There was no other opposition in the primary, so Kefauver moved on confidently to the general election; he defeated his Republican opponent by a 3-to-1 margin, and was off to Washington with Nancy. He was thirty-six years old, ambitious to move into larger arenas, and quietly confident that this would not be a dead end.

As if to put a seal on this, in 1942 Nancy gave birth to the child which they had eagerly desired for six years. They called the girl Eleanor, but she announced her preference for the name of Lynda; then and later, Estes was a devoted (if often absent) father, and if his daughter preferred it, Lynda she would be.

Even as a freshman among 435 members of a body which did not take kindly to those whom it regarded as upstarts, it did not take long for Kefauver to make himself felt. He was quiet, he was mannerly as always, and he sought out the earthy advice of Speaker William Bankhead of Alabama ("Work on your mail") and the practical advice of his fellow Tennesseean, Secretary of State Cordell Hull ("Take plenty of time to decide how you will stand, and never let your constituents down"). But he did not hesitate to speak his mind, and he chose his targets—Congressional reform and the protection of public power and the small businessman—with care as well as with instinctive sympathy.

By dint of careful fence-mending at home, using such devices as sending a certificate of congratulation to every graduating senior in his district, he was returned to Congress in 1940 with a better than 2-to-1 victory. Now he was freed, at least provisionally, to carry forward his fight for the causes closest to his heart.

Despite its spectacular success, TVA was under subtle and indirect attack from the private power companies. One of these, by subsidizing the Chattanooga *Free Press,* had managed to kill off TVA's champion, the *News,* for which Kefauver had written more than one incisive piece. What was more, the cagy old Tennessee Democratic Senator, Kenneth McKellar, was playing both ends against the middle (the middle being the consumer and other beneficiaries of TVA's varied social services), by voting for TVA appropriations— but also introducing legislation that would have returned TVA to the domination of politicians and their private- power supporters.

McKellar was involved in a nasty battle with David Lilienthal, TVA's nonpolitical and enormously able chair- man, over just this issue. Through an appeal to his fellow Southern Senators, and by misrepresenting as a personal attack against him Lilienthal's request that TVA be per- mitted to hold on to its unexpended balance for operating expenses, McKellar was able to jam through the Senate his proposal that TVA be required to ask Congress for money every year.

But he had not reckoned on Kefauver's doggedness. The Congressman took to the House floor in May 1942 and led off the fight for TVA with an impassioned defense of the agency; joined by such Congressmen as John Sparkman and Albert Gore, he sent McKellar's proposal down to defeat after weeks of sustained effort. When, several weeks later, McKellar returned to the offensive in the Senate with a simi- lar campaign, and added to it a proposal that TVA headquar- ters be shifted to Washington from Knoxville, to Kefauver the reasons were all too obvious: "No man can attack the evils of centralization, red tape, and remote control," he said on the floor, "if he has voted to remove the management of the TVA power system from the Tennessee Valley to Washington." And once again he won.

The year 1944 was punctuated by another cheerful event. In November the Congressman was once again returned to Washington with a 3-to-1 victory.

The fight to protect public power did not leave Kefauver unscarred. According to the Chattanooga *News-Free Press,* he was "an irresponsible, dangerous, opportunistic radical," and when he did get elected to the Senate he was received by Kenneth McKellar not merely as a rival, but as an enemy.

Still, his other aims—Congressional reform and protection of the small businessman—were far less likely to attract great support, either in Congress or among the public at large. That did not deter him. With the aid of Dr. Jack Levin, he pulled together his unheeded suggestions for reforming Congress—suggestions which have acquired a new urgency in the 1970's—into a book entitled *A Twentieth-Century Congress.*

The press was prompt and lavish in its praise. "Mr. Kefauver, the principal author in this collaboration," wrote the New York *Times,* "is the progressive, hard-working young representative from Tennessee. Long a student of events at both ends of Pennsylvania Avenue, he speaks with the authority of the active practitioner. This is a sober, temperate study." The New York *Herald Tribune* said it was "excellent," the Philadelphia *Bulletin* called Kefauver "one of the ablest, best-informed, and most public-spirited members of Congress," and the *Saturday Review* noting that Kefauver had a long list of things he wanted done to strengthen Congress, observed: "It is a healthy thing for the citizens to worry about Congress: it is especially healthy when one of the most distinguished and useful members of Congress does the worrying."

Dr. George Gallup wrote to Kefauver, "What the country actually needs most, in my opinion, is more men like yourself in Congress who are able to think of the machinery of government in a constructive way." Perhaps the measured words of the country's distinguished historian, Charles A. Beard, meant most of all to Kefauver: "This volume deals with a question of vital interest to every American citizen. How can our Federal machinery be revamped so as to strengthen representative democracy? Critical and constructive, it describes shortcomings and perils in current practices and presents critical proposals for reform."

But if we want a truly long-range perspective on Kefauver's proposals for governmental reform, we ought to turn to Thomas Kuchel of California, who served in the Senate with Kefauver:

In the middle of the Second World War [Kuchel said of Kefauver in 1963] he fought as a member of the House for a resolution to permit Cabinet officers to come before the full body on a regular basis and submit to questioning on the activities of their departments. At an early date, he demonstrated that not only should Congress be responsive to the people but that the executive should also be responsive, or at any rate, respond to Congress. He never lived to see adopted this or many of the other reforms he proposed in his desire to make Congress responsive to the needs of the people; perhaps most of us will never live to see that day. But if that day should ever come, it will be

due to the diligence and the faith of men like Estes Kefauver.

I was honored repeatedly over the years to coauthor
with him and others in both parties a constitutional
amendment to revise the long-archaic electoral college
system so that it might reflect the will of the people on a
proportional basis. Some day, Mr. President, that too shall
come to pass, and much credit will be due to the long and
untiring efforts of the late Senator from Tennessee.
Through years of public hearings he aroused the informed
opinion of our Nation, those in the universities, those in
journalism, those in public life—to the need for this
change so that no longer would the will of our citizens be
frustrated by the election of a President who had not received the support of a majority of the people: an event
which has occurred more than once in the history of our
Republic. He once described the outmoded electoral college as a loaded pistol pointed at our system of government.
"Its continued existence," he said, "is a game of Russian
roulette. Once the antiquated procedures trigger a loaded
cylinder, it may be too late for the needed corrections."

More than thirty years after Kefauver's "loaded cylinder"
statement, with the country uneasy about the potential
ability of demagogues like George Wallace to paralyze the
electoral process and force one Presidential candidate or
another to come to him for support, the New York *Times*
was reminding its readers of Kefauver's prophetic warning.

But of all his serious interests during these (for him)
comparatively quiet wartime years in the House, it was his
concern for the protection of small business that was to prove
most significant in the great years that lay ahead, even if he

was able to achieve little as an individual Representative and member of the House Small Business Committee. For in the course of his service as chairman of a subcommittee investigating concentration of economic power in the United States, he did more than simply urge wartime aid to such small businessmen as auto dealers and meat producers (squeezed by the wartime economy, by black-market operators, and, most of all, by big business) : he fought for housing legislation, price control, and anti-inflation legislation.

At the end of 1947, he rose on the floor of the House to denounce as "a phony" a bill supposedly designed to help stabilize commodity prices, but actually permitting voluntary price agreements among sellers. "I defy any member of this House," he said, "to cite a single illustration of a conspiracy by big business which resulted in lower prices to the consumer. Yet, we are now asked to enact a law based upon the assumption that this is the ordinary outcome of such conspiracies. The incredible is becoming the fantastic, and the fantastic is becoming the law."

He had been doing his homework most carefully on the entire question of monopoly legislation, in consultation with the chairman of the Federal Trade Commission and Dr. John Blair, chief economist for the Commission. Night after night he studied the complex problems, mastering them thoroughly, and thus beginning a close association with Blair that was to flower years later in a series of historic Senate investigations.

Emanuel Celler, Chairman of the House Judiciary Committee, and dean of the House, was to say many years later,

Behind the soft voice and gentle manner of Estes Kefauver lay immeasurable strength. He was not afraid to tackle the big job, to take on the giants of industry, or the masters of crime. He did it without bluster, without threat, and without arrogance. I recognized in him the intellectual strength combined with a gentleness that made him unique. Listening to Estes then, it would have been difficult to predict that he could capture the hearts of millions of our people—so withdrawn and reticent did he, at times, appear.

Yet that was precisely what he was to do. In 1946, thinking mistakenly that Eleanor was to be their only child, Estes and Nancy had adopted a little boy, David. By 1948, with an established family and an established political base, he felt in his bones that the hour had struck, and it was time for him to make his big move.

four ☆ Moving on Up

☆☆☆ One day in the summer of 1970 a group of prominent people got together for lunch at the Tennessee Club, a
fine old building on the corner of one of the main squares in
Memphis. They had come at the invitation of Edmund
Orgill, hardware merchant and former Mayor, for the purpose of reminiscing about the great campaign of 1948, in
which Estes Kefauver was elected to the Senate and broke
the power of the Crump machine. Long before the luncheon
was over the men—together with Mrs. Frances Coe, a sophis-
ticated civic leader who, with two other Vassar alumnae, had
led what was derisively called "the daisy chain for Kefauver"
—were deep in discussion of the days when the city they
loved had been under the absolute domination of one man,
and of how another man had come along to help them free
themselves from that domination.

It is hard for people who have not lived under tyranny to
imagine the daily lives of those who did—and unhappily
still do, in all too many parts of the world. In democracies
people are thought to be free to keep themselves free, and
to throw out anyone who would attempt to abridge their
freedoms. But things are not always that simple. For over
thirty years before the 1948 Kefauver campaign, the city
of Memphis, in the words of John Gunther, "had not really

28

functioned as a democratic community. A whole generation grew up without fulfilling the first and simplest duty of
citizenship, that of exercising political choice."

Those who gathered at the Tennessee Club in 1970—
lawyers, journalists, a doctor, businessmen, a housewife—had
been part of that generation. They reminded each other,
sometimes with laughter, sometimes with a bitterness hardly
dimmed after the passage of more than twenty years, of how
they had lived at the whim and caprice of Boss Crump.

Perhaps the last of the big-city bosses to run his show absolutely unhindered, Crump had been running not just
Memphis, but the entire state. This was no small feat, for
Tennessee, like Gaul, has traditionally been divided into
three parts: East Tennessee, the hill country that was traditionally not only Baptist but Republican since the Civil
War; Central Tennessee, the state's "midwest" farm area;
and West Tennessee, always the most Southern-oriented—
Memphis, after all, is only a few miles from the Mississippi
line.

People used to say that the Delta (the Deep South of
cotton plantations and Negro field hands) began in the
lobby of the Peabody Hotel, an ornate old heap in the heart
of Memphis, only moments from the Tennessee Club. To
those who got together there in the summer of 1970 that
meant, among other things, that while Memphis Negroes
had voted for many years, they voted en bloc the way Boss
Crump wanted them to. They were simply loaded into
trucks and delivered to the polling places, with no attempt
even to conceal that their votes were being bought by the
head.

It was degrading to the blacks, to the whites who stood by
and watched, and to the entire state, for it was a key factor

in maintaining one-man rule and periodically killing off any attempt by good-government people to take their destinies into their own hands. In a state with a vote that usually ran to about 400,000, 260,000 of them Democratic, Crump needed only a little over 130,000 to run the Democratic party and consequently the entire state. He was always sure of 100,000 votes, with 60,000 of them concentrated in Shelby County (of which Memphis is the county seat). Memphis, more than 40 per cent black, had the largest proportionate Negro population of any Southern city—so Crump's absolute control of their votes was essential to his dictatorship. Since you had to pay a poll tax (which many Negroes could not afford) to vote in Tennessee, Crump paid their tax and thus bought their votes. As John Gunther put it, "the poll tax was the chief single element serving to perpetuate the Crump regime." In addition, since the polls closed an hour *later* in West Tennessee (which is on Central Standard Time), Crump always knew how many votes he would have to deliver there to overcome big margins already recorded in East Tennessee.

What was Crump's regime like? It wasn't just that you saw, with your own eyes, people being paid two dollars to vote right. It wasn't just that, using long paper ballots instead of voting machines, the Crump men knew (by means of such devices as ink spots and torn ballots) exactly how you had cast your "secret" ballot. It wasn't even that the courthouse was completely dominated by the machine, or that people were afraid to stop and talk to each other on the street. What was probably worst was that, as a result of all these things, people were inclined to go along with the machine.

By and large, the business community supported Mr.

Crump. Wasn't he giving Memphis "good" government? Didn't the streetcars run efficiently and cheaply? Weren't graft and corruption down to a minimum?

So what, if you couldn't hire a hall to make an anti-Crump speech? So what, if you couldn't find a printer who would dare to make an anti-Crump poster for you? So what, if the poll tax was used as a device to demean and degrade Negroes? So what, if the children flocked to Mr. Crump's annual picnic and caught firecrackers that he tossed to them, under banners reading THANK YOU, MR. CRUMP?

You went along, even if inside you felt sick to your stomach, ashamed of yourself for not doing anything about the political dictatorship, and in fact for profiting from its continued existence.

Crump had gotten in the habit of winning elections as early as 1910. By 1927 he had a death grip on the state, and in the thirties and forties he reached his apex. Although he was a vegetarian and a teetotaler, he could not resist the use of strong language, threats, and vituperation against those who had the temerity to oppose him or his hand-picked stooges. Readers of a new generation may well be reminded of certain demagogic politicians in the 1970's.

In 1946 Edward Carmack had had the nerve to oppose Crump's man, Senator McKellar, in the Democratic primary. He was promptly labeled, in flamboyant newspaper ads throughout Tennessee, as a donkey and a vulture; cruel, treacherous, and venomous, with "no more right to public office than a skunk has to be foreman in a perfume factory." The language was typical Crump. It was typical too that Crump should employ it against political opponents (who always wound up being beaten anyway by as many votes as were necessary), and also against those journalists courageous enough to support his opponents or simply to criticize him.

Thus Crump began a letter to Ed Meeman, able editor of the Memphis *Press-Scimitar*: "Your stupidity at times defeats the cold cruelty and cunning evil with which you seek to inject in your news articles and editorials." To Silliman Evans, publisher of the Nashville *Tennesseean,* he sent his poison-pen letters by private messenger, in order not to risk prosecution for violating the postal laws! In the latter he labeled Evans "a foul mind and wicked heart," and Jennings Perry, editor of the *Tennesseean,* "unworthy, despicable, a venal and licentious scribbler . . . with the brains of a quagga," as unintelligent as one would have to expect of "a wanderoo." The *Tennesseean's* political columnist, Joe Hatcher, he labeled "a filthy, diseased mind," full of "ululation." The latter three Crump grouped together as "mangy, bubonic rats, yellow to the core."

Spiro Agnew might well envy Ed Crump such words as "quagga," "wanderoo," and "ventosity" (of which Crump accused Meeman). But he would do well to study his history: for when Mr. Crump trained his verbal guns on the mild and gentlemanly Estes Kefauver, who must have seemed a sitting duck to the old political boss, the backfire was so strong that it destroyed the Crump machine and all but propelled Estes Kefauver into the White House.

One Sunday afternoon early in 1948 Congressman Kefauver came to the Peabody Hotel on a scouting trip, to see how his Senatorial aspirations would be received in West Tennessee. "The most impressive thing about him to me," recalls Dr. Henry B. Gotten frankly, "was his ability to remember my name—not an easy one—at the end of the meeting, particularly since he was so notoriously absentminded."

The people were receptive, Kefauver found, but many of them warned him—as did his own father—that he would get nowhere bucking the bosses, and that if he wanted to supplant Senator Tom Stewart he would do best to soft-pedal attacks on bossism. Stewart, however, had been working hand in glove with his cohort Kenneth McKellar to sabotage the TVA program, and to Kefauver this meant he would have to take on both Stewart and his backer, Boss Crump.

Then came one of those odd, unpredictable turns which make politics so endlessly fascinating. Crump decided to dump Stewart and throw his presumably decisive support to Judge John Mitchell. But Stewart, to everyone's surprise, declined to be dumped, and announced instead that he was remaining in the race, making it a three-cornered one.

Now the question was: Who would be the gainer? Would Senator Stewart, as the well-known incumbent, manage to defeat the Crump machine, or would he instead split the anti-Crump forces that had been preparing to unite behind Kefauver and thus ensure the continuation of old man Crump's political domination?

In the circumstances, as Kefauver later wrote,

I decided to find as accurately as possible how matters stood with the voters. I asked a representative of a famous research poll to determine the voters' preference among the candidates. The findings, only 13 per cent for me, were so shattering that I did not show them to my campaign manager because I did not want to discourage him further. I sat in my office alone, trying to decide whether to get out of the race. Only recollection of my mother's advice finally decided me to stay in the race and do my best to overcome the obstacles in the way.

I ran scared. I discussed the campaign issues for sixteen or seventeen hours a day in some three hundred towns, cities, and hamlets, visiting each two or three times. I pronounced my name clearly, with a strong accent on the first syllable, and was encouraged to find that an odd name, once learned, is more easily remembered than a plain one.

As if his low standing with the voters as a Senatorial possibility in the summer of 1948 were not enough, Kefauver found himself attacked by the Republican press as well as by Crump for being "Communistic." His old enemy, the Chattanooga *News-Free Press,* accused him of having voted down the line, on issue after issue, with the American Labor Party Congressman from Upper Manhattan, Vito Marcantonio, whose name was a dirty word not only to right-wingers but to many middle-of-the-road Americans as well.

Despite their dissimilarities in background and allegiance, there was in fact one aspect of their political lives that Kefauver and Marcantonio did share: service to their constituents. Marcantonio was so admired by the voters of his district—for the most part poor and humble—because of his tireless attention to their personal and often painful problems; they could not have cared less that his position on foreign policy faithfully followed that of the Communist party paper, the *Daily Worker.*

One of the facts that outraged the *News-Free Press* was that on its form chart of Congressional candidates' voting records, the CIO rated Vito Marcantonio as 100 per cent, and Estes Kefauver as 81.8 per cent. Commenting on the charge, Marcantonio remarked, quite correctly: "Kefauver and I have never worked together closely for the passage or defeat of any legislation. On foreign policy we are in absolutely opposite camps . . . although I have respect for Kefauver's honesty, personal integrity, and ability, I would say that at rock bottom he is a conservative."

Kefauver himself refused to apologize for his record, much less to back away from the issue. Buoyed by Nancy's surprise pregnancy and the arrival of a second daughter, Diane, he took to the offensive. He telegraphed to the press: "Marcantonio has always aligned himself with the Democratic party in the House. In other words, my vote fairly closely parallels that of the Democratic leadership. It appears that your paper does not like the Democrats."

He chose the steps of the Monroe County courthouse, where he had spent so many fascinated afternoons as a youngster listening to the spellbinding judges and lawyers, to make a forthright statement on the entire question.

My course of action as a friend of the common man has gained for me much abuse. Some call me too progressive, others too liberal. Some have even hinted that I am a Communist, but no one dares make that charge except by innuendo. That is a coward's way. But I am undisturbed. Mislabeling the bottle has never changed its contents. If to believe in the right of every man to the good life, to the utmost liberty, and to the most complete happiness is to be a radical, then I expect the description fits most of us.

Throughout his Congressional career, Kefauver had voted consistently against Federal "loyalty" programs, contempt citations, and investigative programs, and particularly against the continuation of the House Un-American Activities Committee, believing them to be invasions of the basic rights of the American citizens (this consistent record was to be thrown in his face more than once during the McCarthy era) . So it was all the more surprising when Representative John S. Wood of Georgia, a former chairman of the House committee investigating "un-American" activities, rose on the floor of the House to join others in praising Kefauver and wishing him well in his Senatorial campaign. Said Congressman Wood: "As a member of the Un-American Activities Committee and one of its former chairmen, I wish to state for the record that the forthright stand my colleague, the gentleman from Tennessee, has always taken in defending and preserving the civil liberties of citizens has in my opinion tended to strengthen the fight against un-American activities."

What had enraged Wood, as well as thirty-three other Congressmen who arose to defend Kefauver, was an advertisement that appeared on June 10, 1948, in every daily newspaper in the state of Tennessee. ESTES KEFAUVER ASSUMES THE ROLE OF A PET COON, read the headline. Once again, the text picked up the charge that Kefauver was not only a follower of "the CIO line," but "a darling of the Communists." The section that was to make history, though, was the paragraph that read:

"Kefauver reminds me of the pet coon that puts its foot in an open drawer of your room, but invariably turns its head while its foot is feeling around in the drawer. The coon hopes, through its cunning by turning its head, he will deceive any onlookers as to where his foot is and what it is into."

The tone was unmistakable; but as if to ensure that no doubt should be left in anyone's mind, the text was boldly signed: E. H. CRUMP. Once more, the Boss had spoken—and this time the battle lines were drawn.

Within a day, Kefauver headquarters was fighting back:

"The coon is a clean animal; it washes its food before eating. The coon is an American animal; it is found nowhere else in the world. The coon is a courageous animal; it can lick its weight in dogs any day.

"A coon has rings around its tail," Kefauver observed dryly, "but this is one coon that will never have a ring through his nose." He added, "The coon is an easy animal to domesticate, but a mighty hard little critter to put a collar on."

But the clincher came when the candidate announced defiantly, "I may be a coon, but I'm not Mr. Crump's pet coon."

Editor Ed Meeman had been told by Kefauver, when he first decided to make the Senate race that spring, that he would fight Crump. Meeman was appalled. In a memorial column, he recalled years later the advice he had given to candidate Kefauver: "One candidate after another has made Crump the issue and the negative policy has failed. Just come to Shelby County and present yourself and your program, appeal to the people for their votes as you have a right to do. Don't fight Crump, but if Crump fights you, as I think he will, fight back."

The method Kefauver chose to fight back was as simple as it was dramatic. He arose before the large crowd that had gathered to hear him in Memphis' Peabody Hotel and began to speak; in the middle of his talk, he reached down into the paper bag at his side, pulled out a coonskin cap, and clapped it on his head.

The effect was electric. Meeman, who had warned against

such sensationalism, had to admit that he had been quite wrong about its impact. Wherever he went, Kefauver wore the coonskin cap, and wherever he went he was greeted not simply with laughter, but with applause. Crump's attack had backfired, and so badly that it was to result not only in victory for the upstart but in the destruction of his supposedly impregnable machine. And the greatest irony was that all this took place in the heart of Crump's fortress, Memphis itself. For in conjunction with Meeman and lawyer Lucius Burch, a group of leading Memphis businessmen, impressed by Kefauver's courage, banded together to gain him support in the quarter where it had been least expected.

Crump fought to the end, and with the only weapons he knew. He ran more full-page ads, and he challenged Ed Meeman to debate the question: Is Estes Kefauver a Communist sympathizer? Typically, he suggested that the loser should leave Memphis for good. Kefauver handled this one neatly by asserting that he himself would be happy to debate that proposition, but with Crump's candidate.

To the very end, the people of Memphis feared that the primary election would be stolen from them. "After all," as one of the original group recollects, "I had friends who were afraid to stop and talk to me on the street. So we did nothing to kill the rumor that the FBI was interested in our primary situation, and would be watching for law violations."

"Still," says another, "it was our Kefauver poll watchers who really had it tough on that primary day. They had to suffer every kind of intimidation and seduction, even to being offered whiskey by the Crump people. You know, this was the first time in the memory of any of us that anyone had even *tried* to have poll watchers in Shelby County."

It went down to the wire with the anti-Crump people hopeful, but uncertain. "Remember," stresses Mrs. Coe, "we couldn't find more than two hundred people in all of Memphis who were willing to put their names to anti-Crump, pro-Kefauver advertisements."

"The moral angle," says editor J. Z. Howard, "was quite simply that an anti-Crump man became a marked man. In those circumstances, some mighty good people went along with the machine."

On primary day Kefauver voted in his home precinct in Chattanooga, but promptly flew west to walk the streets of Memphis, shaking hands as he went—a foolhardy move, his supporters thought. One of the poll watchers was David Brown, now a judge, but then a young lawyer: Brown stood glumly watching firemen and policemen as they hauled in Crump's usual truckloads of working-class and Negro voters.

He had no way of knowing that, once inside the privacy of the booth, many would vote their consciences. Although the AF of L leadership went along with Crump, Kefauver had met with the CIO leaders, whom Crump had run out of town, and swung them to his side. He had also met with Negro community leaders—it was the first time in anyone's memory that a political candidate had done so—and earned their respect.

When the votes were counted in crucial Shelby County, Kefauver got 27,000 of them (usually the opposition had been able to figure on about 2,000!) to Crump's 40,000. That 27,000 gave Kefauver the margin he needed to win all of Tennessee. He was a Senator and Crump was through.

In John Gunther's opinion, three main reasons accounted for Crump's downfall and collapse: "Disintegration within the machine itself (state employees were tired of having to

kick back percentages of their salaries), liberalizing elements at large, and the personality of a stunning new arrival
on the national scene, Estes Kefauver."

About ten years later that stunning new personality was
asked by a professional humorist for an assessment of his
own brand of humor. He wrote back:

> The coonskin cap had its own particular place in my
> political campaigns. Its purpose at that time was to inject
> some humor, and it would be out of place any other time
> when the same necessity was not present. Then, however,
> there existed in Tennessee a political machine which was
> the subject of fear among a great many people. The coon-
> skin cap got the people laughing, and one is not afraid of
> a man or a machine while laughing at him.

five ☆ Looking at the World

☆☆☆ For the people of Tennessee the biggest immediate benefit of Kefauver's smashing 1948 Senate victory was the resulting collapse of the Crump machine. Robert Tillman, a lawyer and labor leader of Memphis, made this quite clear when he warned a Memphis crowd one July evening of that crucial year: "Somewhere along the line the torch of freedom has been trampled in the dust of Tennessee, and we have no one to blame but ourselves.

"There is a man in town," he went on, "who belongs to no civic club as far as I know—at least, he attends no meetings—yet he controls the civic clubs. Although neither he nor his sons went to public school, he controls the PTA and the school board.

"He is not a lawyer—and neither are his sons—but he has controlled the bar association. He holds no union card—and neither do his sons—but he's done a pretty good job of controlling the labor unions.

"I ate at the same swill barrel," Tillman confessed, "but I got out." And he added, "Kefauver's big fault was that he didn't ask permission when he got ready to run for the Senate."

When Kefauver got ready to run for the Presidency four years later, the story was to be the same. But first we must understand clearly another element in his stunning 1948 victory.

If the key element in that victory was the voter of Memphis and Shelby County, the key element in Shelby County was the "marriage of convenience," as Dr. Gotten calls it, between two groups of amateurs who got behind Estes Kefauver in defiance of Boss Crump. One group, as we have already seen, decided that the hour had struck for them to stand up and be counted for good government. The other, led by Lucius Burch and Ed Meeman, was far more concerned with international problems and the concept of Federal Union (a federated government of the Western democracies), a local chapter of which they had established in Memphis following a talk by its founding spirit, Clarence Streit.

In April 1948 Kefauver was conferring at the Peabody Hotel with Meeman and Burch and Edmund Orgill about the possibility of the latter's heading a Memphis for Kefauver Committee. Suddenly from Madisonville came news that Phredonia had had a cerebral hemorrhage. Estes rushed off, carrying with him a gift from Lucius Burch, a copy of Clarence Streit's *Union Now*.

Under ordinary circumstances Kefauver might never have gotten around to reading the Streit book—he was a busy Congressman, deep in the most critical campaign of his career. But during the lonely hours in the hospital, sitting quietly at the side of his dying mother who had written him so many daily letters, he immersed himself in the book that had already caught the imagination of the Memphis idealists. When he finished it he was sold on its thesis, and accepted Streit's analysis and what seemed to him a sensible solution to the problems of the age.

After his mother's funeral he told the Memphis group that he would support their cause in the U.S. Senate; they decided that a real live Senator on their side would be far better publicity for the cause than their running around individually to various service-club luncheons and church meetings.

In order to get the essential support of Edmund Orgill [Meeman was to write] Kefauver had to convince Orgill he was for Atlantic Union, for it was only to advance this cause that Orgill was willing to enter politics.

Kefauver did pledge himself to advocate Atlantic Union. But, if he had been merely a politician, how easy it would have been for him to make one speech, introduce a resolution for it, say, "I'm sorry, but you see the time is not ripe," and abandon the effort.

But Estes had become convinced that organic union of the free, democratic nations of North America and Western Europe was necessary to overcome Communism. He worked for it, fought for it. When, in campaigns, demagogues attacked him for it, he did not flinch. He was a speaker in demand throughout the country, he could choose his own subjects, and often he chose to speak in behalf of Atlantic Union.

He was the principal architect and the leading American figure in organizing the NATO Conference, which has been meeting every year since 1955, the Atlantic Congress of 1959, and the Paris Conference of 1961 . . . Kefauver's exposure of gangsters and his fight on monopoly were spectacular. But I will wager that he will have a great place in history as the statesman who, more than any other, pioneered in behalf of the federation of the free.

What was the idea that so captured Kefauver's imagination? In the fateful year of 1938, Clarence Streit was League of Nations correspondent for the New York *Times* in Geneva. After seeking a publisher for his *Union Now* for five years without a taker, he had become convinced that it was essential to rush it into print, somehow. By his reckoning, World War II would start in August or September of 1939 if the Atlantic democracies did not meanwhile start to confederate. So he decided to print a few hundred copies at his own expense and circulate them among the Western leaders he had come to know in the ten years he had been covering the League of Nations.

Working with his wife in the print shop of an Italian anti-Fascist exile in a tiny Franco-German village, Streit single-handedly chose format and paper, designed the cover, title page, and book, and helped with mechanical layout work.

By dint of last-minute corrections and insertions, he had succeeded in making the book as up-to-date as a weekly magazine. With the Munich "Peace in our Time" agreement between Hitler and Chamberlain (and the sickening feeling spreading throughout the West that a Second World War was now inevitable) Streit's book had suddenly become enormously timely. Regular trade editions appeared in New York and London in the spring of 1939; the New York edition went through seventeen printings, followed by numerous other editions.

One reason for the book's enormous circulation and impact was the simplicity of its thesis. Streit believed that security against aggressive war-making powers could not be achieved by isolation or by adherence to such powerless forums as the League of Nations. Rather, peace could be secured if the Western democracies—the United States, the

British Commonwealth, the French Republic, the Lowlands, Scandinavia, and the Swiss Confederation—would agree not merely to military pacts, but to organic union in an unchallengeable body. The bonds of friendship forged during the wartime alliance among most of those nations served as further evidence to Streit—and to an increasing body of supporters, persuaded by his book and his speechmaking—that his plan would be as feasible in the post-Hitler world as it had been when the German dictator was still bullying the democracies into surrender.

In addition, the break-up of the Soviet-American alliance after World War II and the ugly confrontation of the two superpowers seemed to Streit to prove his case: Atlantic Union was more essential than ever.

This is not the place to examine in detail the strengths and weaknesses of Streit's argument, which gained acceptance among influential men on both sides of the Atlantic, if not among ordinary citizens. The point here is that, once Estes Kefauver was convinced of the reasonableness and the morality of that argument, he was not going to be deterred by the fact that it was unlikely to become a popular or a vote-getting issue.

When he came back to Washington as a Senator with his growing family (Gail, the last Kefauver child, was born in 1950) , Kefauver had dreams of being tapped for the Foreign Relations Committee. He was not the first freshman Senator to harbor such ambitions. After all, now that America was the greatest world power, foreign affairs had become a matter of pressing concern to every American family, and Senators who could speak with authority on international matters were more likely to gain nationwide attention than those who specialized in particular aspects of domestic affairs. Kefauver did not get the appointment he was hoping for. But that did not prevent him from speaking out very quickly on the international dilemma as he saw it.

Even before his elevation to the Senate, he had inserted into the *Congressional Record* in the spring of 1948 a speech by Edmund Orgill in support of Federal Union, prefacing it with the observation that "to sustain a lasting peace, steps other than the European Recovery Plan are going to be necessary."

Within weeks, he included a Federal Union plank in the formal announcement of his candidacy for the Senate:

> I have studied the matter very closely. I am convinced that the one real way that we can have peace in the world is to join in a kind of federation with the other freedom-loving peoples. . . . I feel that the statesmen of these democracies should work toward this program, just as the statesmen of our Union worked toward building thirteen States into the Federation which grew into the great United States of America. . . . It is going to take work, a lot of prayerful thinking, and moral and religious re-generation. But it is not only possible. It must be done.

On July 11, 1949, the freshman Senator took the floor during the debate on ratification of the NATO alliance. "I shall vote for its ratification," he announced, "only because I see it as a necessary interim measure, a measure that will gain the time needed to explore in peace a far more promising prospect—the possibility of eventually uniting the democracies of the North Atlantic by our own basic Federal principles into a great Atlantic union of the free."

In his address he harked back to the American experience,

as he had done when he announced his candidacy for the Senate.

Much has been said of the United States Constitution in the discussion of this treaty, but it seems to have been forgotten that our Constitution is itself a foreign policy. It originated as a basic foreign policy to govern the relations of sovereign States with each other, and with all the rest of the world. It began as an answer to the kind of problem we and the other Atlantic democracies now face, how to secure our liberty without another war. It began when an attempt to solve this problem by an alliance— the Articles of Confederation, in some respects much closer and stronger than the treaty before us—had failed to work even among thirteen States whose people had more bonds in common than the twelve signatories of the North Atlantic Treaty.

Faced with the dangers of war, depression, unemployment, and inflation despite their Articles of Confederation, the delegates of the earliest Atlantic democracies met in a convention at Philadelphia in 1787—met, to quote one of them, William Paterson of New Jersey, "as the deputies of thirteen independent, sovereign States." There they worked out our Federal Constitution as the solution to their common problem in foreign policy, as the basis of their relations with each other. . . .

Twice in our lifetime [he pointed out sharply] we have sought to secure our freedom without war. Twice we have failed. Twice the boys have had to save the day, make up for their elders' lack of vision, wisdom, self-sacrifice, and courage. And twice we have seen that merely to win by war is no enduring answer, even though the surrender be unconditional and we occupy Tokyo and Berlin. Twice we have seen that all the sacrifices of our youth cannot secure our freedom without another war if their elders remain unwilling to sacrifice dangerously narrow, selfish views, disastrously outmoded concepts, fail to tackle the problem with the vision and courage that success requires.

In the modern world, he insisted, old notions were no longer good enough.

When Senator Andrew Jackson came to represent my own State of Tennessee in this hall in 1823, he had to make the trip of 860 miles on horseback, all except the last leg of it, which he made by ship, and even that short leg took him five days. Now I can make that trip from Tennessee in fewer hours than it took Andrew Jackson weeks.

If wisdom counsels us not to abandon lightly policies that have long proved good, it tells us too, not to cling to them blindly when they are producing worse and worse disasters.

Suiting his action to these words, fifteen days later Kefauver introduced the first Atlantic Union resolution in the Senate on behalf of twenty Senators. Nor did he quit when the resolution died in the 1949 Congress. In 1951 he reintroduced the same text, this time on behalf of twenty-seven Senators. The Korean War had broken out, and as he told the people back home, in explaining to them why he was stepping down as chairman of the Senate Crime Investigating Committee, "Tennessee boys are dying on foreign battlefields and I believe this plan I proposed may provide the answer we pray for. Therefore, I consider it my bounden duty to turn my efforts and time from local and national crime to international crime."

In the interim, a Senate subcommittee had been holding hearings relative to the United Nations, Atlantic Union, World Federation, and other resolutions. On February 15, 1950, Kefauver took over the questioning of two State Department officials who were attempting to explain why the Department opposed calling an international convention to consider all the problems that would have to be resolved before there could be an unprecedented Federal Union of the world's democracies.

I have to admit very reluctantly that I am terrifically disappointed with the attitude and the lack of imagination of the State Department [Kefauver told the two officials, one of whom, Dean Rusk, was to become Secretary of State a decade later]. I think the State Department, Mr. Chairman, also doesn't apparently realize that the people are getting awfully tired of paying the expense of a cold war when they don't see any great something that we are seeking or trying to arrive at. . . . We are going to have to realize and take into consideration the attitude of our people in wanting some great exploration, some star to hitch our wagon to, and also the attitude of people in the other parts of the world.

Clarence Streit was present through all of the dialogue that ensued. Thinking back on it twenty years later, he called it "the sharpest cross-examination I ever heard Estes make. I didn't expect anything as good as this, since he had to do it off the cuff."

That cross-examination gave a foretaste of the quiet but devastating method that was very soon to make him the terror of criminal and corporate executives alike.

MR. HICKERSON: Our feeling, sir, is that the convention is premature, that there must be . . . study and understanding and a meeting of minds.

SEN. KEFAUVER: Who is the State Department to say that you think it is premature?

MR. HICKERSON: You asked our views here.

SEN. KEFAUVER: Yes; we ask your views, but don't you think the American people are able to decide for themselves whether they want to go into a Federal Union with other Atlantic democracies, whether they want to accept the recommendations of a convention?

MR. HICKERSON: I frankly, sir, don't think there has been sufficient expression on the part of the people of the United States that they are ready to embark on such an undertaking, nor do I think, sir, that there has been a sufficient expression in the other countries concerned.

SEN. KEFAUVER: I don't know who you have been talking to, but I think . . . people . . . know that military alliances never work over a long period of time. Military alliances such as the Atlantic Pact have never worked, and federations have never failed. So that maybe it depends on who we talk to. Here you say: "Are the American people prepared to do so? To what extent? To what kind of authority? By what process?" The only way in the world that I know we can find out whether the American people are prepared to do so is to have a convention to do nothing but explore the possibilities. . . . Do you want to give the American people a chance to do that?

A moment later Kefauver swung his attention to Dean Rusk, who expressed the State Department attitude that exploration of Federal Union be done on a private rather than on a governmental basis, since the latter would imply a political commitment.

SEN. KEFAUVER: Mr. Rusk, . . . there is no political commitment to accept what comes out of the exploration until the people themselves make the commitment, is there? Every witness has testified to that.

MR. RUSK: There is no political commitment on the part of the United States to accept the result of the study, but there is a political event brought about by summoning such a group for a study of this subject which is not just neutral.

SEN. KEFAUVER: I want to say if the State Department is afraid in the conduct of its foreign policy to explore along the lines that saved this Nation and made us the strongest union, well, then, I am afraid we are being very weak in our efforts, Mr. Rusk. . . . Do you think the formation of Benelux and the breaking down of customs barriers between those three nations was in violation of the principles and purposes of the United Nations?

MR. RUSK: No, sir, I don't.

SEN. KEFAUVER: Do you think the effort that is going on at Strasbourg, to try to have a Western European Union, is in violation of the purposes of the United Nations?

MR. RUSK: No, sir.

SEN. KEFAUVER: Then you must not think that any peaceful effort to try to bring democratic countries together so that they can trade with one another better and to do in one effort all of the things that we are trying to do in various efforts could be in violation of the purposes of the United Nations, do you?

MR. RUSK: That doesn't follow, sir. If we try to get together with the nations of Western Europe to make a fundamental redistribution of political power, we will create very deep chasms between themselves and ourselves and raise issues which we could do without at a time when we need maximum unity.

SEN. KEFAUVER: Chasms with whom, Mr. Rusk?

MR. RUSK: With the other members of the association whom you would call together to work these things out with. In other words, when you get into such questions as responsibility for money, responsibility for trade, responsibility for protection, for arms, you raise a great many conflicting interests which, if not worked out in great detail ahead of time, would divide rather than unify.

SEN. KEFAUVER: Let me say in that connection that we have gone along this far without raising any questions with those people we are doing business with on the ground that we are afraid of hurting their feelings.

MR. RUSK: It is not a question of hurting feelings, Senator.

SEN. KEFAUVER: Don't you think the best way to divide the responsibility about who is going to do what and to unify in a common effort is to get together and get the thing out on the table and see what you have and where you are going to go? Isn't that the way you have to do business?

MR. RUSK: That is correct, sir, and if the Congress and the people and the President have come to the conclusion that this is the way in which we move, then we can do that, but in that process, we are going to have to determine whether we really mean what we say on this thing. For example, if we are going to try to deal with the dollar-gap problem, we are going to have to accept a great many goods into this country, which we are not now willing to accept. For us to pretend that we wish to talk seriously to other people about a thoroughgoing federation without having met that kind of an issue among ourselves would be deluding people.

SEN. KEFAUVER: You don't know whether we are ready to meet the issue or not, but you are trying to give the answer for the American people. . . .

Whether or not the American people were willing to meet the issue of moving away from nationalism and toward international federation, they were not to be given an opportunity of discussing, much less asserting. Presidents, Secretaries of State, Secretaries of Defense, generals, admirals were all so bemused during the 1950's and 1960's with proving to the entire world that America was ready to drop everything from paratroops to high explosives on those who opposed them, that they had little time (and less eagerness) to offer to the world the kind of peaceful prospect that Kefauver had assumed was a part of the American heritage.

"There has been no general acceptance of the idea of an Atlantic Union," Senator Eugene McCarthy observed many years later, and then added about Kefauver, "but his efforts have had an effect by widening the vision of Congress and the people."

NATO as a military instrument did not particularly inspire Kefauver. But "seeing in it much more than a mere military alliance," as Senator Hubert Humphrey put it, he sought to give it political content by helping found the NATO Parliamentarians' Conference, of whose political committee he was chairman.

It was no wonder that Clarence Streit wrote to Senator Wayne Morse about Kefauver:

> From the start of his Senate career in 1949 when he was chief sponsor of the Atlantic Union resolution, he remained a prime mover for Atlantic unification. He reintroduced that resolution twice. Then because he felt it would help to have the leadership come from a member of the Foreign Affairs Committee, he stepped aside when the resolution was introduced the last time, and helped energetically from the ranks to secure its adoption in 1960. . . . When Estes entered the Senate there was no talk I heard there of even such things as "the Atlantic community." It is a measure of his courage, vision, and steadfastness that such talk is now commonplace. . . .

No one would claim that Estes Kefauver was an innovator or a contributor of original proposals to aid in the resolution of international problems. Yet he had something which we might consider even more precious—idealism, courage, and steadfastness. Perhaps his friend Elmo Roper expressed best the effect of these qualities on Kefauver's view of the world:

> Over the years he never wavered in his support of Atlantic Union, publicly or privately. Called "a nigger-loving one-worlder" in the middle of a hot political campaign, he took the epithet calmly in stride and retreated not an inch from his convictions. Everything he ever told me he would do, during the long battle for Congressional acceptance of the idea of an Atlantic Citizens Convention, he did. In a profession of easy promises, he kept every one.

Yet a very good case could be made that the first thing one should mention in connection with Senator Kefauver was in his vision. Many years ago he realized that rivers, mountains, and oceans, color of the skin and religion were unnatural boundaries for governments. To let any of them assume the unnatural importance they have come to have in this twentieth century was to invite—at worst—continued wars and—at best—continued costly rivalries. In a world shrunken by fast transportation and faster communications and where men know how to destroy centuries of civilization in minutes, some stronger cement was needed to bind men together. To Estes Kefauver that binding cement was a belief in the dignity of every human being. On that foundation, he would have built a broader, more enduring government than this planet has ever seen.

six ☆ Dishes Go Dirty and Detroit Goes Wild

☆☆☆ During his early months in the Senate, Estes Kefauver was far from exclusively concerned with global problems. Troubles a lot closer to home worried him deeply. He had tried, without much luck, to make peace with his old foe, Tennessee's cranky senior Senator, Kenneth McKellar, and was frankly relieved when the aging man was replaced by Albert Gore, a friend and an ardent supporter of TVA.

Kefauver took his stand at once for civil rights, and made it clear—as he had in the House—that he was unalterably opposed to the poll tax. For his maiden speech—John Blair still regards it as "one of the best researched speeches on the Senate floor in decades"—he spoke up scathingly on the techniques used to kill off civil rights legislation, concentrating his fire particularly on the filibuster.

Coming from the lips of a Northern Senator it would not have been a courageous speech, although it would still have been a good one. But for a Senator with a Southern drawl to oppose his racist colleagues, for a newcomer to support a Rules Committee recommendation that debate be limited so that civil rights bills could be acted upon—that was the next thing to treason, and Kefauver was to pay dearly for his quickly announced independence.

Also in 1950 he had the pleasure of fighting through to a successful conclusion, with Congressman Emanuel Celler, the bill that was to bear their name. "The fruit of a five-year drive," as the New York *Times* described it in a tribute to his dogged persistence, the Kefauver-Celler bill was characterized by its co-author as legislation which "forbids the acquisition of one firm by another where the effect may be substantially to lessen competition, or to tend to create a monopoly."

In his posthumously published study of monopoly, *In a Few Hands,* Kefauver added the following retrospective comment on the bill's results:

> A number of actions by both antitrust agencies have been instituted under this provision, and several have been successful in halting mergers that would have been harmful to competition. In addition, it must be remembered that, in the area of antitrust enforcement, the full impact of the law is never entirely discernible. In this respect, the effectiveness of the antitrust laws has frequently been likened to a floating iceberg; only a tiny portion protrudes above the surface and is visible to the human eye. No one can guess how many potential mergers reached the discussion stage and were finally abandoned by the parties because of the Clayton Act amendment, nor how many were summarily dismissed on this ground before negotiations had entered the preliminary stages.

"We both felt," Congressman Celler observed, "that economic concentration was an evil that had to be fought and resisted."

Wary of Big Business and its lobbyists who served as guides, advisers, and buddies to many of his new colleagues,

Kefauver unhesitatingly jumped in to attack the "basing point" bill, a piece of legislation carefully designed by monopolistic interests to be so confusing and complicated that no ordinary citizen could be expected to figure it out. And he tacked on an amendment to a Big Business bill that effectively killed off its attempt to weaken the antitrust laws.

But all the time he was searching hungrily for a forum in which he could function before a substantial public. Fighting for the public interest as a legislator was all very well; before he was through his voting record would compare favorably with any Senator's. But both his legal background and his political instinct sent him looking for an opportunity to set to work on a large-scale investigation.

In the beginning of 1950 he decided that he had found an opening wedge. Given his innate suspicion that Big Business tended to become bigger at the expense of the ordinary man, it struck him that the time was ripe for an examination of similar tendencies in the criminal underworld. Was there really such a thing as a crime syndicate? If so, did it parallel Big Business in its influence over lawmakers and law-enforcers? Was there actually a movement toward monopoly in the world of the rackets—gambling, hijacking, dope, prostitution—and if so, was there anything Congress could do to protect the public?

It was not as easy as one might have thought to get authorization for such an investigation. Kefauver's resolution to have the 81st Congress investigate organized crime had to be passed on by the Judiciary Committee. The chairman of that committee was Pat McCarran, whose home state of Nevada was owned at least in substantial part by a consortium of gambler-businessmen and their criminal cohorts.

As a member of the Judiciary Committee, Kefauver kept after the reluctant McCarran, who finally agreed to an investigation, after newspapers began asking why one should be held up.

At this point Colorado's Senator Ed Johnson, Chairman of the Interstate and Foreign Commerce Committee, decided to claim jurisdiction. If the press was going to interest itself in such a probe, why shouldn't his committee claim responsibility—and credit? The issue had to be compromised, and it was, with Kefauver's suggestion that a special committee be formed with members from both committees.

The Democratic party accepted the compromise, but Kefauver was still not out of the bureaucratic woods and into the public arena. Four months later he was still waiting for approval from the Senate. Finally, he had to break in to the debate on the foreign-aid bill over the objections of the Senate Majority Leader, Scott Lucas of Illinois. Like McCarran, the irresolute Lucas was finally persuaded that an investigation of crime might be a good thing—after a number of newspapers began asking why he didn't think it would be.

This touchiness made the entire probe uncertain down to the final vote—a 35–35 tie, due to the Republicans who wanted it solely under the sponsorship of the Judiciary Committee—which was finally resolved by Vice President Alben Barkley's tie-breaking vote in favor of the Kefauver plan.

Now he had his Special Committee to Investigate Crime in Interstate Commerce, soon to become known to millions of Americans as the Crime Committee, or the Kefauver Committee. It was going to make him an overnight television celebrity, as familiar on home screens as Milton Berle, Red Skelton, or Jackie Gleason.

The existence of organized crime was not something that

had sprung up from the nowhere in the 1950's. In the city and the country, in the courthouse and the countinghouse, as well as on the frontier and the range, the American tradition extending back in time through the nineteenth century was often one of either no law at all or of contempt. what law there was. In 1929, in a book entitled *Our Business Civilization,* the historian James Truslow Adams had characterized Americans as "a population already the most lawless in spirit of any in the great modern civilized countries. Lawlessness," he observed with a kind of mournful realism, "has been and is one of the most distinctive American traits."

Despite the periodic cleanup efforts of individual reformers and organized groups of indignant citizens, the nation seemed always to sink back into an apathy that was perhaps Kefauver's most difficult roadblock. People just didn't seem to care—at bottom, perhaps, because they couldn't bring themselves to believe that anyone in public office was objective and honest enough to get at the truth and demonstrate that something could be done about it.

On the other hand, Kefauver did have a weapon—the authority to bring together into one task force all governmental law-enforcing and regulatory agencies—that had never before been available. The top mobsters had for years been able to operate unmolested in a kind of legal no-man's-land. Both state and local officials (those that had really wanted to do something about it) had been frustrated in their efforts to prosecute criminals operating across state lines. What was more, they discovered that they could not get much help from the various federal agencies: The FBI had no power to investigate gambling and the Treasury agents had no power to crack down on the gambling syndicates beyond collecting taxes on their slot machines.

But the Kefauver Committee now had the authority to borrow both personnel and facilities from any of the Federal agencies. Starting with his own staff of about ten investigators, Kefauver was able to tap the resources of FBI agents, Secret Service men, postal inspectors, narcotics agents, Bureau of Internal Revenue agents, and intelligence officers of the armed services. His committee turned too to the Federal Communications Commission, which requested telephone companies to keep a permanent record of the details of all long-distance calls, the basic tool of both bookie and numbers racketeers. From the Department of Justice, and its attorneys all over the country, the committee obtained a mass of information about a list of 150 underworld characters, including such notorious types as Frank Costello, Joe Adonis, Ralph Capone, Mickey Cohen, Marty Krompier, Joey Rao, Meyer "Socks" Lansky, Jake Lansky, Waxey Gordon, Charles Fischetti, "Trigger Mike" Coppola, and Anthony Garfano.

Now Kefauver and his four fellow Senators were ready to swing into action. They were an oddly assorted group, particularly the gentle, scholarly Tennesseean, his New Hampshire Republican colleague Charles Tobey, who came on like a New England Sunday school teacher, and the aggressive committee counsel, New Yorker Rudolph Halley, who had served on Harry Truman's war investigating committee. Methodically they moved from city to city, holding hearings, building the record.

"Senator Kefauver does not specialize in dramatic flourishes," the *Christian Science Monitor*'s correspondent reported from St. Louis. "He is a tall, cool, soft-spoken gentleman with great personal dignity. He does not shout. He does not rant. He does not wax sarcastic. The procedure in the room reflects his moderation."

None of this seemed calculated to arouse much public excitement, even though Kefauver was as anxious as the next politician to get himself across to the country at large. But then something happened which it is hardly likely he could have foreseen. Blair Moody, himself a former newspaper reporter and member of the Senate, told the story in *Holiday* magazine, in an article entitled "The U.S. Senate":

> Often a lucky break will bring into prominence a solid Senator who merited fame all along but somehow had not achieved it. Senator Estes Kefauver of Tennessee is a prime example. He had long been at work to build a more effective code of laws to combat crime. He had written a thoughtful book proposing ways to streamline Congress, and had quietly moved into the front rank of internationalists in the Senate.
>
> Kefauver's solid achievements did not get him major attention, however, until an alert Detroit reporter, Allen J. Nieber, thought of putting the crime hearings on television. Shortly before the Kefauver Committee was due in Detroit, Nieber flew to Cleveland and got the Senator's consent to televise the hearings over his paper's station. The result was sensational. Dishes went dirty and Detroit went wild. So did the rest of the country after the commission hit New York. Kefauver's name became a household word.

It had been one thing to read about faceless mobsters testifying before the committee as it moved from city to city. It was quite another to see them—and their political and "law-enforcement" buddies—on your television screen, squirming and wriggling under a barrage of questions from

Halley, while Estes Kefauver, as the *Monitor* put it, scared the hell out of them.

"Smiling Jim" Sullivan, Sheriff of Dade County (Miami and Miami Beach), lost his smile when he was asked how he had boosted his net assets of $2,150 at the beginning of his four-year term to more than $100,000 at its conclusion. He kept up to $12,000 at a time rolled up in a blanket. . . .

Bookie John F. O'Rourke, operating out of West Palm Beach, decided to tell the committee the details of his having been taken for a financial ride by Mickey Cohen.

The former police chief of Miami Beach testified that he hadn't wanted to "get involved" with bookmaking. When Kefauver asked whether that hadn't been part of his job, Lieutenant Short replied, "I knew what hot potatoes were."

"I never tried to find out certain things," testified Detective Walter Ahearn of Saratoga Springs, New York, after acknowledging that he made extra money by hauling a gambling joint's receipts to the bank. Saratoga's chief of police got ten dollars a day for bringing cash from the bank to the racetrack; but he didn't know anything about the city's gambling joints. Sheriff Walter Clark of Fort Lauderdale testified that he had grown rich while in office. Sheriff Hugh Culbreath of Tampa testified that there was a bookie operation in his own office. Sheriff John Grosch of New Orleans, so his wife testified, kept $150,000 in cash in an attic strongbox.

The bigger the city, the worse the stench. In Philadelphia policemen were being paid off at the rate of $152,000 a month. In Chicago, Police Captain Thomas Harrison got a $30,000 gift from a man in the racing wire-service business, "because I was his friend and a sort of bodyguard for him." To which Kefauver replied acidly: "He was a nice fellow."

In Chicago, Captain Harrison was not unique. Arthur Madden, Treasury agent in charge of the Chicago Intelligence division, estimated that at least forty police captains were worth more than a million dollars each. Captain Dan "Tubbo" Gilbert, chief investigator for three state's attorneys between 1932 and 1950, was one of the most notorious of the lot, "an elder statesman in the field of political corruption," in the words of Ovid Demaris, author of *Captive City*. Gilbert was already being worked over in the papers when the Kefauver Committee arrived in Chicago. (The Chicago *Sun-Times*: "All right, Captain Gilbert. Let's look at the record. . . . How about Ernest D. Potts, a precinct captain, killed just before March 30? He was your personal friend. You attended a political meeting with him the night he was rubbed out. He was ambushed gang-style in the vestibule of his home. He was mixed up with gambling all his life. You said you knew him for forty years but couldn't find his killers. . . .")

Demaris' account of what happened next makes lively reading:

> The kiss of death was delivered by a soft-spoken Tennesseean. Senator Estes Kefauver came to town three weeks before the 1950 November elections to preside over the first hearings held in Chicago of the Senate Crime Investigating Committee.
>
> In typical Chicago fashion, a few days before the committee convened, two important witnesses (former Police Captain William Drury and attorney Marvin Bas) were silenced by gang bullets. . . .
>
> Of the hundreds of anonymous letters received by law-enforcement agencies in the wake of the Drury murder,

the following to Kefauver is worthy of attention: "Jake Guzik and Charles Fischetti ordered Bill Drury killed. Guzik sent word to his North Side triggermen Dominick Nuccio and two other Dominicks, and Nuccio supplied three shotguns and .45 caliber pistol for job. After killing, killers returned to Nuccio's saloon and hid guns. Everyone knows the Doms' last names. Now go and get them lined up for electric chair. They have good, crooked lawyers known as BB boys."

One of the first witnesses to testify before the Senate committee was Gilbert's new boss, State's Attorney John S. Boyle, elected in 1948, who was soon confronted with his past. Under prompting by the committee's counsel, Boyle admitted that he once was attorney of record for Trans-American, but denied having any knowledge that it was gangster-owned—it had been written up in the press countless times. "They (Accardo, Guzik, Fischetti, *et al.*) never let me know about it if (they were behind it)," he said. As to the type of people that purchased Trans-American's wire service, Boyle answered: "Pretty high-class-looking people." (Boyle is currently Chief Judge of the Criminal Court.)

On October 17, 1950, Captain "Tubbo" Gilbert was quizzed by committee counsel Rudolph Halley at a closed executive session:

MR. HALLEY: Specifically, it is said around here that you never arrested Capone or Fischetti or Guzik. . . . You have no hesitation and no fear of arresting them?

CAPT. GILBERT: No, I have not. I never saw Fischetti on the streets of Chicago I think but once in my life. I think he was coming out of a show with his wife. He came out with a girl. . . .

MR. HALLEY: Would you say that this long list of unsolved murders and the situation which has prevailed over the last twenty years has been one which through lack of co-operation or lack of coordination of law enforcement has not been what it should be?

CAPT. GILBERT: No. I will say this to you, Mr. Halley. I have never violated my oath of office. When these gangsters go out and kill they are as precise and detailed in their work as an architect. If an architect makes a mistake, that architect can correct the mistake. If a doctor or lawyer makes a mistake, you can dig in the archives and get some help. These men, when they go out to kill, they don't leave nothing. . . .

MR. HALLEY: From the point of view of public confidence . . . isn't it only natural that when people realize that a man in your position has amassed great wealth, and you have rather considerable assets, that they should lose confidence in you?

CAPT. GILBERT: The failure of human nature is that we are prone to believe evil about our fellow man, and especially about a police officer.

Fascinated Americans could hardly help but believe evil. Disgusted Chicagoans turned out almost all Illinois incumbents, including Gilbert (who promptly took off for Southern California) , and far more importantly, Senate Majority Leader Scott Lucas (who chose to believe that Kefauver's exposure of the Chicago mess had been deliberately undertaken to thwart his own Vice Presidential ambitions) , replacing him with Everett M. Dirksen, the flamboyant

Republican orator. Gilbert, so disappointed with fickle human nature, had estimated his net worth at $360,000 (a figure which the committee regarded as ridiculously low). But then his superior, Police Commissioner Prendergast, had already put on a show of ignorance paralleling that of "Tubbo" Gilbert:

MR. HALLEY: Do you know of any evidence or have you an opinion as to whether the Capone group of gangsters or their successors are still operating in any fashion in Chicago?

COM. PRENDERGAST: I have no personal knowledge. I have nothing in my reports to indicate that they are.

MR. HALLEY: Do you have any information at all, Commissioner, about the Mafia?

COM. PRENDERGAST: No. Years ago, of course, I knew a little about the Unione Siciliano. Was that it?

Lawyers joined with police officials in attempting to make a display of their innocence and naïveté. Eugene Bernstein, a former Federal attorney with the Bureau of Internal Revenue had, in the words of Ovid Demaris, "prepared income tax returns for just about every hoodlum in the higher income brackets." He responded to Halley's questioning like this:

MR. BERNSTEIN: The word "gangster" has a different connotation to me than it may have to other people. A gangster is an individual who goes out and, by means of force, duress, obtains sums of money. If you and I go out and do certain things legally, and place funds in his possession without duress, at our own direction, and then he does

something with that, that would not be gangsters. Gang-
sterism is very definitely a form of violence.

MR. HALLEY: A gangster is a man who belongs to a gang,
isn't he?

MR. BERNSTEIN: Then you and I are gangsters. . . .

MR. HALLEY: What gang do I belong to?

MR. BERNSTEIN: We belong to the human race. We belong to
a political party. That may be a gang.

Chicago political figures too, it turned out, not only had
intimate relations with the gang, but were themselves an
intimate part of it. Criminal lawyer and state legislator
Roland Libonati, recipient in 1950 of a gold watch inscribed
by Governor Adlai Stevenson for his work in behalf of the
Civil Service Protective Association, was characterized in the
Kefauver report as a "bosom pal" of top gangster Al Capone.

State legislator James Adduci, with a record of eighteen
arrests at the time of his first election, was best friends with
a key Capone hoodlum, "Dago Lawrence" Mangano.
Adduci explained his friendship with Mangano in the
following words:

MR. ADDUCI: On the primary and election, Lawrence used to
give me a little finances to help me finance my precinct
when I was a precinct captain.

SEN. KEFAUVER: Do you generally accept political help from
gamblers and bookmakers?

MR. ADDUCI: In my precinct I would accept a little finances
from any kind of a business.

By the time the committee reached New York, it seemed
that all of America was glued to the tube, gaping at the

parade of underworld figures who took the stand—wriggling, sweating, and trembling as they had made others tremble. Salvatore Moretti was less grammatical and less polite than Chicago's Prendergast or Bernstein had been, but he was no less incredible under questioning:

MR. HALLEY: Do you know what the Mafia is?

MR. MORETTI: What?

MR. HALLEY: The Mafia. M–A–F–I–A.

MR. MORETTI: I'm sorry. I don't know what you're talking about.

MR. HALLEY: You never heard the word before in your life?

MR. MORETTI: No, sir. I did not.

MR. HALLEY: Do you read?

MR. MORETTI: Nah. As I says before, I don't read very much on account of my eyes.

Perhaps the prime villain to confront the new national hero, Estes Kefauver, was Frank Costello. Regarded by many as the top man in the entire underworld, Costello topped off his elegant wardrobe with a breast-pocket handkerchief which bore his name embroidered on it. But he was not eager to make this public appearance; in fact he requested that the television cameras not be directed to his perspiring— if barber-shaved—countenance. Millions of viewers gazed instead at his manicured fingers, clenched together before him as he denied keeping records, but finally admitted to having some $40,000 or $50,000 in cash in a strongbox in his elegant home.

As if that were not enough, former New York City Mayor William O'Dwyer, who had been shipped off by President Truman to cool it in comfortable exile as U.S. Ambassador to Mexico, blustered his way through questions about why he hadn't prosecuted mobster Albert Anastasia when he had been District Attorney O'Dwyer, what he had been doing during the war in Frank Costello's apartment, and why he had accepted $10,000 in a brown paper bag from a representative of the firemen's union.

In characteristic fashion, Kefauver commented on the testimony of O'Dwyer that it was "A melancholy essay on political morality."

It was more than that. It was a red flag waved before Kefauver's own party. First he had alienated the Southern Democrats by speaking up for civil rights, and against the filibuster and the poll tax. Now he had enraged the big-city machine Democrats, all the way up to the White House, by refusing to back off from revealing the extent of their involvement with crime and criminals.

Governor Fuller Warren of Florida, furious at the revelation that he had gotten campaign contributions from the underworld, went to work on Kefauver within the Democratic party.

Senator Scott Lucas of Illinois, furious at the Chicago revelations, blamed Kefauver for his defeat—and succeeded in impressing upon the Democratic party establishment the presumptuousness of a freshman Senator who would publicly discredit the Majority Leader.

And in the White House Harry Truman, not one to suffer supposed disloyalty to the party whose faithful servant he had always been, waited and bided his time.

Kefauver himself was perhaps somewhat naïve in not seeing this clearly. Engulfed by a roaring wave of public approval, he stepped down from the chairmanship of the committee after eleven grueling months. The road show had kept him all but continuously separated from his wife and the children who—like so many Americans—had been watching him in the living room, before their TV set. He returned home to ponder the impact of the crime investigation on the American people and on his own political future; he came to the conclusion that there was no reason why he should not prepare to run for the Presidency.

He thought too about a number of other matters, as important in their own way as the big decision. A substantial number of columnists, newspapers, and magazines were greeting his handling of the committee hearings with all but unrestrained praise; the careful *Christian Science Monitor* reported to its readers that "there is no doubt that slowly a pattern is emerging which will enable the entire Senate to make up its mind whether Federal laws are needed to curb activities of gamblers." So it came as a jarring shock when personal friends and civil libertarians charged him with violating the civil rights of some of the gamblers who had been called to testify.

To be sure, there had been moments like the baiting of a former Philadelphia numbers operator, Louis J. Crusco, by committee counsel Halley:

MR. HALLEY: I think you are the worst liar I ever heard in here. . . .
MR. CRUSCO: I have been a sick man. I take spasms.
MR. HALLEY: You look as though you were about to have one.
SEN. KEFAUVER: Let's get on with the investigation.

But then there had been the moment when Saint Louis betting commissioner James Carroll, objecting to the blinding lights and the television cameras, had cried out: "This whole proceeding outrages my sense of propriety!" And Kefauver had responded by threatening Carroll with a citation for contempt.

His loyal friend Elmo Roper recalled asking Kefauver, one day when they were sitting quietly and drinking scotch, "Why are you doing this crime inquiry?"

To which Kefauver responded, "In Tennessee I'm known as the Great Investigator. I think it's a good thing for me to have an investigation in an election year—and this is a safe one."

It was an answer that did not please Roper, particularly when Kefauver demanded, "How do you reconcile being so helpful, raising campaign funds and all, and turning on me as you are now?"

Roper pointed out that he had never criticized Kefauver in public, but always would to his face, and that as a Senator he ought to acknowledge some of the ethical problems not just of criminals but of those who were investigating them. "I judge people by Roper's Law for Senators," he told Kefauver. "If they vote as I would 65 per cent of the time, I'm pleased. If they vote as I would 75 per cent of the time, I'm delighted. If it's 90 per cent, I worry—because then I get afraid that they won't get elected."

Kefauver laughed, but he saw a profound truth in what Roper was getting at, and passed the story all around the Senate. What was more, he thought hard about the basic moral question of infringing on the constitutional rights of witnesses testifying before Congressional committees. Publicly he acknowledged his mistake in ordering Carroll to testify before television cameras, and he took to the Senate floor to admit the error. He offered several resolutions that revealed his own sensitivity to violations of human rights at a time when most public figures were yielding to the demand for easy assaults on those who were vulnerable and unpopular. One resolution aimed at establishing strict rules of procedure for investigating committees; the other at prohibiting Congressmen from making derogatory remarks about anyone without notifying the person in advance of the attack and offering him equal space for rebuttal in the Congressional Record.

> Here on this floor [the Senator reminded his colleagues] the Senator from Wisconsin introduced the names of a number of persons associated with the State Department against whom he made various charges. When he had completed naming these persons, he observed, "Some of them"—speaking of the persons he named—"may be able to prove that they are neither security nor loyalty risks.". . . The unfortunate thing has been that charges made on the Senate floor, sometimes without proper foundation in fact, and charges made before committee hearings, sometimes likewise devoid of foundation, have the tendency to convict, in the minds of the public, those persons against whom such charges are made.

To underline his conviction that Congressional investigations had gotten out of hand, Kefauver sent a letter to Lyndon B. Johnson just before Johnson took over as Senate Majority Leader in 1954: "I have been aghast . . . at the excesses to which the various committees of Congress have gone in the fields of the so-called subversive investigations. They have made us all look ridiculous by their headline-grabbing tactics."

Journalist Sidney Shalett, in an introduction to *Crime in*

America, the book that Kefauver put together out of the hearings, may have summed up the investigation most succinctly: "His message was nothing that was particularly new. . . . But Kefauver patiently dug out facts about the stinking mess, and he told the story to the public that made all but the most cynical want to get out and do something about it." Senator Tobey said at one of the final hearings: "This man, Estes Kefauver, had in his heart a need of decency in America." And Shalett added, "The people heard him, saw him (thanks to the youthful television industry) , and liked him."

Kefauver's substantive conclusions, embodied in his committee's interim reports, foreshadowed his later concern with the dangerous power of monopoly. "Criminal syndicates in this country make tremendous profits," said the third interim report, "and are due primarily to the ability of such groups and syndicates to secure monopolies in the illegal operations in which they are engaged. These monopolies are secured by persuasion, intimidation, violence, and murder."

The Mafia, the committee was convinced, had an important part "in binding together into a loose association the two major criminal syndicates as well as many minor gangs and individual hoodlums throughout the country." It summarized its findings about the Mafia in five major points that were substantially in agreement with the opinion of experienced police officers and narcotics agents.

But the voice of the committee's chairman, and his spirit as well, can be heard in its conclusion: "Modern crime syndicates and criminal gangs have copied some of the organized methods found in modern business. They seek to expand their activities in many different fields and in many different geographic areas, wherever profits may be made."

Except for his subsequent chairmanship (in 1955) of a subcommittee investigating juvenile delinquency, Kefauver was finished with the subject of crime. As for the larger problems of monopoly and Big Business, he had barely begun.

But first there was the question of whether he could translate his popularity into votes. He had decided to try to become President of the United States.

seven ☆ The Biggest Prize of All: "The Basic Issue of Power"

☆☆☆ In the spring of 1951, when Estes Kefauver stepped down from the chairmanship of the Crime Committee and announced straightforwardly, "There is a distinct possibility I may run for President," Harry S Truman had been in the White House for six years.

The sudden death of President Roosevelt as the Second World War was drawing to a close had propelled the little-known Missourian from an inconspicuous incumbency as Vice President to the center of a world stage on which he sat with such giants as Churchill, Stalin, and de Gaulle. Struggling to cope with power and great decision-making, Truman found himself presiding over a Democratic party that seemed to be splitting into irreconcilable fragments.

On the left, he was deserted by Henry A. Wallace, his predecessor as Vice President and the man he had appointed Secretary of Commerce. Wallace felt that the country was being whipped into a warlike frenzy against its former ally, the Soviet Union, by the military and the industrialists. On the right, Truman was deserted by Southern Democrats who regarded him as a traitor to White Supremacy and a captive of the big-city machines, the big unions, and the blacks.

At the approach of the 1948 Presidential election, Harry Truman's stock was so low that even within his own party he was being urged not to attempt a hopeless race. With Wallace nominated by the Progressives and Strom Thurmond by the Dixiecrats, almost no one was willing to bet a nickel on Truman's chances for re-election. His Republican opponent, Governor Thomas E. Dewey of New York, who had been wildly overmatched four years earlier in his campaign against President Roosevelt, was now so confident of victory that he went to bed on election night convinced that he had been designated as the next occupant of the White House.

But Truman had waged a tough and unyielding campaign. While Dewey coasted, hardly exerting himself, Truman ran hard, day and night, and succeeded in conveying a sense of himself as a courageous underdog, fighting the good fight for the ordinary American against an incredible array of enemies.

In victory Truman was—only naturally, perhaps—cocky and somewhat overbearing. Both the Progressive and the States' Rights parties faded away as the forties faded into the fifties, and Truman reasserted Presidential control over the Democrats. By 1952 he alone had the power to decide whether to accept nomination for another term. If he chose not to run—which was most likely, since he had already served nearly seven years—he also had the power to name the Democratic nominee.

This was not such a prize as it might have seemed. While Kefauver was traipsing around the country crime-busting, American boys were dying far away, committed by President Truman to the defense of a regime in Korea which was confusing if not meaningless to them. Their families at home supported the military action against the North Korean invasion, particularly since it was a United Nations struggle, with the military participation of many allies and under the American leadership of General Douglas MacArthur. But pro-war sentiment weakened as the conflict dragged on, and the nightmare of a large-scale land war with Communist China became frighteningly real. Truman fired the aggressive General MacArthur, but appeared unable to bring to a conclusion a war that no one seemed truly eager to fight, much less to win.

In addition, Truman had surrounded himself with a set of cronies whose virtue was distinctly secondary to their clubhouse morality. American voters have usually been willing to tolerate a certain amount of skulduggery by their elected officials—and ready to throw them out when the corruption became too blatant. A man of unimpeachable integrity and courage, Harry Truman seemed positively unwilling to detach himself from his hangers-on, and tied for good and all to the corrupt city machines that had elevated him from the obscurity of small-time storekeeping to the most powerful office in the world.

Such was the situation when Estes Kefauver came to the White House in January 1952 to inform the President of the United States that he was interested in the job for himself.

Kefauver had reason to believe that Truman would look upon him favorably as a successor. He had upheld the President's wishes on both domestic and foreign issues. In Seattle he had spoken up for the Presidential policy of limited war in Korea, against the line of MacArthur and his right-wing allies at home who said that the war should be expanded and carried to the Chinese mainland. In Congress he had fought hard for Truman's Fair Deal program and stood firmly with the President in opposing the infringement of civil rights. He had voted in favor of amendments to the Equal Rights amendment, to provide that no current or future rights of women should be impaired by passage of the Equal Rights Amendment to the Constitution; moreover, in 1950 he had reintroduced his own amendment to set up a commission on the Legal Rights of Women to investigate any discrimination against women on the basis of sex.

In the summer of 1949 Kefauver had raised his voice in the Senate in defense of TVA Chairman Gordon Clapp, who had been declared "unemployable" by nameless accusers in the Army. "I think it is a travesty of justice," Kefauver said, "that men of his caliber are smeared in such a manner on the unexplained charges of officials of the military government. Men in the public life of our country should enjoy some protection from smear methods."

The following year, Senator Pat McCarran introduced a so-called Internal Security Bill which would presumably protect the country from the "Communist menace"—a perennially popular American issue, and one which would plague the country in the years immediately ahead.

"Were it not for the insidious threat of Communism and were we not in the very shadow of World War III," Kefauver asserted during the debate, in the midst of the Korean War, "no thinking American would ever consider asking Congress to enact laws to control the thoughts of any of its citizens." A week later, after having pointed out that the bill would permit unwarranted prosecutions, without due process of law, he took the floor once again to remind the country that both Mussolini and Hitler had given their people "internal security." He said flatly, "We will never defeat and destroy the Communist movement by adopting totalitarian methods of our own," and he voted—along with only six other Senators—against the bill.

President Truman vetoed the bill. And only ten Senators —Kefauver conspicuous among them—stood with the President to uphold his veto.

What Kefauver had not counted on, however, was the President's conviction that the Crime Committee's spotlighting of corruption had given the Republican party its Number One domestic issue for the forthcoming campaign. Truman had not forgotten Kefauver's insistence on bringing out the unhappy fact that Frank Costello, kingpin of American racketeering, had contributed $2,500 to the Democratic National Committee; or that the Democratic mayor of New York City had been bailed out of a scandal-ridden situation and appointed by Truman himself as Ambassador to Mexico; or that the Senate Majority Leader, Scott Lucas, had been defeated for re-election in Illinois at the peak of his career, in 1950, as a direct result of the uproar surrounding Kefauver's exposure of Police Captain Gilbert as a grafter. Kefauver had tried unsuccessfully to placate Lucas by asserting that he had deliberately taken the testimony of "the world's richest cop" in executive (that is, private) session, but that a Chicago newspaper reporter had posed as a Federal employee in order to gain possession of the transcript and leak the story.

None of this, though, was even discussed at the Kefauver-Truman meeting. Kefauver confined himself to pointing out the obvious, that if President Truman decided to seek re-election, he himself would not go for the nomination.

The President said that he had not yet made up his mind, but that in any case the party needed new blood. As an old hand at winning national elections, he wound up by suggesting: "Play up your victory against the Crump machine. The people will like that."

Encouraged, Kefauver left the White House convinced that President Truman would not stand in his way. Within the week, he had made the formal announcement that he was going to seek the Democratic nomination for the Presidency of the United States.

He was determined to have his name entered in every single state primary, with the exception of Minnesota, where Senator Hubert Humphrey had already agreed to switch the delegation he controlled to Kefauver in the event that Truman chose not to run.

The first primary, as everyone knows who recalls Senator Eugene McCarthy's historic effort against President Lyndon Johnson in 1968, takes place in New Hampshire while the snow is still on the ground. Estes and Nancy Kefauver betook themselves to New England, such unfamiliar territory that the Tennesseean made at least one speech in Vermont before he realized that he had strayed over the state line.

He had strayed over the political line too, as he discovered when the angry Democratic machine placed the name of President Truman on the ballot in addition to his own. Taken aback, he offered to withdraw from the primary if the organization would withdraw the President's name, and leave the entire matter up to the New Hampshire delegates.

But the die had been cast. The party chiefs decided that the time had come to cut the six-foot-three campaigner down to size; and the gamblers against whom he had been inveighing began to quote odds of 3 to 1 against him.

Kefauver had the choice of quitting or pushing on. With his effervescent wife at his side, he plugged ahead in the same dogged manner which had always proved so effective in Tennessee but until now had been untested elsewhere.

When primary day was over the Senator had won a clear majority—an astonishing victory over the President—and gained undying enmity for this rash act of presumptuousness.

In the months that followed, Truman did not chance a repetition of the New Hampshire humiliation. He kept his name out of the more than dozen subsequent primaries, but not his opposition to the upstart. Senator after Senator was trotted out to oppose the Tennesseean, and each in turn went down to defeat as Kefauver stumped their home grounds and demonstrated his amazing personal popularity.

In Illinois, Scott Lucas took charge of the campaign against the man whom he now regarded as his mortal enemy. With the aid of a $40,000 slush fund from the Democratic National Committee, he promoted a high-pressure write-in campaign for Governor Adlai Stevenson, who had been extremely reluctant to become involved in the rough and tumble of national politics. The effort was wasted: The Governor got some 50,000 write-ins, while the Senator received close to 500,000 votes.

Years later, Charles Tyroler II, who had been closely involved with Kefauver during the 1956 campaign, spent a brief quiet vacation with him in Florida after Kefauver had delivered an address for State of Israel Bonds in Palm Beach. As they chatted, relaxed and alone, Tyroler asked him what he thought had been his biggest political mistake in the past.

"When I beat Adlai in the primary in 1952," Kefauver replied, "I should have stopped the primary campaigning. I should have gone back to Washington to my Senatorial work."

But he did not. The momentum seemed too great to

reverse, and he rolled on, from state to state, committed to proving his popularity even though primary victories in themselves had never been decisive in swaying the politicians who had the final say when convention time arrived.

After New Jersey and Illinois came Massachusetts and Nebraska and Wisconsin. But the Florida primary gave the Old South its chance. Governor Fuller Warren, like Scott Lucas in Illinois, had not forgotten his humiliation when the Kefauver Committee had served up the state's hoodlums and crooked sheriffs—to say nothing of the contributions he had accepted from the underworld. He published a 21-point statement attacking Kefauver's fitness for the Presidency and demanding that the Senator reply personally.

Since Warren declined an invitation to a debate in Jacksonville, Kefauver went directly to the Governor's Tallahassee office. As the dumbfounded state employees stood staring, he marched down the corridors, shaking hands as he went, moving with his great loping stride into the Governor's office. But Warren had left—and Kefauver had made his point.

This kind of bold amiability had worked well for him back home. Boris Kostelanetz, who had known Kefauver since the forties, when he had been a special assistant district attorney investigating crime and had joined forces with Kefauver in the crime exposé, recalls a story told him by a distinguished anti-Kefauver lawyer: "The man was trying an important case in a Tennessee county district court. Suddenly in walked Kefauver—he shook hands with the judge, the plaintiff, the district attorney, the jurors, with everyone! and then calmly walked out. Who did he think he was, God?"

Kefauver's boldness gained him publicity in Florida, to be

sure, but it did not gain him the state's delegates. The voters, given the choice between him and Richard Russell, his Georgia colleague who stood for the values of the Old South, went for Russell.

It was an omen that Kefauver might have heeded. But the same day he won a smashing victory in Ohio, which helped erase the Florida defeat, and he took California by a huge margin. South Dakota and Oregon were easy, and when he captured a third of Alabama's delegate votes, he felt that he had demonstrated massive popularity even in the Deep South. So he returned to the White House for another session with the President.

This time their meeting was briefer, and the President's smile was cooler; Truman limited himself to the observation that, as head of the Democratic party, he was concerned that the primary fights should not leave scars "that would not be healed after the convention."

That sounded like neutrality, but since—no matter how many primaries you won—the President personally controlled several hundred delegate votes, Kefauver grew uneasy when he heard rumors that Truman was lining up votes against him. Back he went to the White House for one last call. This time the President was not merely cool but cold, especially when Kefauver said in departing, "I hope, Mr. President, that you will not interfere at the convention."

Still, he had reason for optimism. Coming to the Chicago convention with fourteen victories in sixteen primary campaigns, with the public opinion polls showing him the most popular candidate, and with a larger bloc of pledged delegates than any other candidate, he truly believed that the professionals would have to bow to the will of the people. (Charles Caldwell, his administrative assistant during the last years of Kefauver's life, puts the matter very succinctly:

"The pols never quit hating him, and he never quit trying to win them over.")

In a 1952 column Marquis Childs summed up his popularity by observing it was not surprising that Big Business "should encourage the belief that Kefauver is a slightly comic fellow in a coonskin cap. . . . Here in Washington the cynical explanation for his success is his great buildup as a crime-buster on the nation's television screens. But the real reason may be the sheer novelty of a man who is saying something out of his mind and out of his heart about the basic issue of power and its use and abuse in mid-century America."

Kefauver had also been concentrating on the very practical matter of ingratiating himself with voters not just in Tennessee, not even just in the states where he could win primary victories, but throughout the country.

Boris Kostelanetz, who spent six weeks in 1952 as Kefauver's New York State chairman, remembers how they worked to gain the friendship of delegates already pledged to Governor Averell Harriman. "Wherever we went, there was a shadowy figure writing down names and addresses. And everyone got a letter. Terrific staff work!"

That kind of staff work had made Kefauver unbeatable back home; now it was starting to pay off in the country at large.

If I talked to a delegate from, say, Schoharie County, I'd explain that we were not in competition with Ave—but he might think about coming to Kefauver if it turned out in Chicago that Ave wasn't getting anywhere. That night a note would be typed out to him on Kefauver's letterhead: "Dear Mr. Jones, Boris tells me of the pleasant visit he had with you. I want to assure you that my children, like yours, love to go on picnics (or whatever else of a personal note could be introduced) . Averell is a great American, but the nice things you said are gratefully appreciated by me. Come to see me in Chicago."

Kostelanetz would send the letters to wherever Kefauver was; the Senator would sign them and mail them off in batches. It was a technique of saturation, and it worked. When Kefauver checked into his Chicago hotel suite, he was swamped with delegates simply wanting to shake his hand and chat for a few minutes.

They came to him, though, not simply in response to cleverly composed letters, but because he had struck the chord. It was that once-in-a-lifetime thing, the politician who—without being a great orator, a great wit, or a father figure—managed to express what people wanted not just for themselves but for the country. He made them feel too that while he was willing to work within the system—indeed, was proud of his practicality—there were certain things he would not do, certain deals he would never make.

One such occasion, although it was not to be made public until years afterward, came in the midst of this unusually tense convention. The first ballot showed Kefauver leading with 340 votes to 273 for Adlai Stevenson, 268 for Richard Russell, and 123½ for Averell Harriman. To achieve the 616 required for the nomination, he needed to find 276 more votes.

Frantic telephone calls were being made, meetings held in steamy hotel rooms, deals offered and rejected. Kefauver had arrived in Chicago dog-tired from the cross-country grind of rounding up delegate support for his candidacy. He was accustoming himself to catching catnaps aboard airplanes, putting on a pair of blinders and the bedroom slippers he always carried in his briefcase. But the pace was still murderous, rushing from a banquet to a private meeting, from a session with local politicos to a radio show, from a TV broadcast to a waiting car headed for one more airport.

Now, bleary-eyed and sleepless, he had to huddle with the representatives of his rivals for the biggest prize of all—and to make quick decisions that might change not just his future but that of the entire nation.

At what point does a man dedicated to change, and to fighting for equity and equality within the system, decide that he can compromise no further? In the past, Kefauver had shown that there were certain basic issues—public power, civil rights—on which he would not temporize inside the state of Tennessee. Always he had gotten away with it; indeed, that was the basis for his already legendary reputation for political courage. It was one thing to speak up for human rights against property rights in Brooklyn, but to speak up in Tennessee!

Now he was suddenly faced with a gift of substantial Southern support—*if* he would shift his ground on the Tidelands oil issue. For many years oil has been the source of some of America's greatest fortunes; one reason for this has been the unique tax benefits available to investors in the oil industry, another, the lack of Federal control over oil taken from the sea (it has always been simpler for Big Business to control state legislatures than the Congress in Washington, for obvious reasons).

Early in the convention Governor Allen Shivers of Texas, who spoke for a good-sized bloc of Southern delegates, held a secret meeting with Estes Kefauver. If Kefauver, who had always supported Federal supervision of offshore oil reserves, could see his way clear to compromise, if he would promise that as President he would not veto a Tidelands oil bill returning offshore oil within a three-mile limit to state control, a deal could be worked out.

Kefauver understood that because of its special history, Texas had a stronger claim to that oil than any other state. But he told Shivers that he could make no such pledge.

He was given one more opportunity to make the pledge, and responded by displaying what Douglass Cater has called a "capacity for lonely action" that served to "place him apart from other Senators in the regard of certain individuals and groups who can be helpful to a man with Presidential ambitions."

In *The Reporter* magazine, Cater recounted

a hitherto secret episode that happened during the crucial second ballot at the Chicago convention when, with Kefauver leading 362½ to 324½ against Stevenson, there were still high hopes at his command center in the Stockyards Inn. Governor Gordon Browning of Tennessee, a close friend who had nominated Kefauver the day before, burst in on the candidate with a message from Governor Shivers. If Kefauver would sign a rather vaguely worded statement promising to give just consideration to the Gulf Coast states in their Tidelands oil claims, Shivers would swing Texas' vote to him and could probably bring along Mississippi's. Kefauver, groggy with fatigue, answered without hesitation, "I can't sign it, Gordon." The deal was off.

We cannot conclude from this that Kefauver was a more noble candidate than, say, Abraham Lincoln, who was not above wheeling and dealing. Or that he would have gained the nomination—and perhaps the Presidency—if only he had decided that he would rather be President than be right. The cold truth is that those who ran the show were implacable in their hostility and in their determination to prevent his gaining control over their organization. It made no difference to them that someone had hit home with a sign above his headquarters proclaiming: NOBODY WANTS ESTES BUT THE PEOPLE.

Sitting in the chair of the convention was Speaker Sam Rayburn, a tough Texan operator who used the power of his position to discriminate against and to deny the floor to the Kefauver forces, particularly their leader, Illinois Senator Paul Douglas. And sitting in the White House was Harry Truman, who had finally decided upon Adlai Stevenson as the man to stop Kefauver.

In the middle of the second ballot, just when it began to look as though the Draft Stevenson move might not be able to stop Kefauver, the President arrived from Washington. He sent his man, Charles Murphy, directly to Averell Harriman with a directive that he withdraw in favor of Stevenson. The deed was done, and victory for Kefauver had become an impossibility.

Kefauver decided that there was only one thing to do. In order to spare any further humiliation to Paul Douglas, who had exposed himself terribly by opposing his own state's and party's governor and the President's choice, and who now lay weeping from the exhaustion of the vain effort, he would go to the floor with Douglas and have the latter announce that all of the Kefauver-pledged delegates would be released to vote for Adlai Stevenson.

But when they walked down the aisle, followed by Harry

Mansfield, they were not recognized by the chair, and were made to sit down quietly at a back corner of the platform. Sam Rayburn, unrelenting to the end, seemed determined to rub Kefauver's nose in it, and did not allow him to take the floor to salvage something for Paul Douglas, if not for himself. Only after the votes were counted was he recognized.

"When Senator Douglas and I came into the convention hall," Kefauver told the delegates, "it was in the hopes that we could receive recognition at that time. I was going to nominate my good old friend Senator Douglas. Of course, nominations were not in order, and it was his plan then to ask that everybody join in supporting Governor Stevenson. Ladies and gentlemen, I have fought a hard fight. We have done the very best we could do."

The next day, after it was all over, the inner circle gathered to choose Stevenson's running mate. Stevenson's first choice was Kefauver, but Truman, Rayburn, Lucas, and the rest were hardly in an appeasing mood. They promptly vetoed the Stevenson idea, and accepted Truman's choice of Senator John Sparkman of Alabama. As for Kefauver, he had nowhere to go but Tennessee, worn out, battered, and sick at heart.

What had gone wrong? Across the country, thousands of his supporters were outraged at what seemed to them to be, in the words of the *Detroit News,* "the result of back room double-dealing and double-crossing to pull the rug from under the people's choice." This feeling, that the "People's Party" (what the St. Louis *Post-Dispatch* called the Democrats) "had ignored the will of the people," was so intense that it all but ensured the switching of many voters to the Republicans—particularly when the latter passed over Sena-

tor Robert Taft in favor of the war hero, General Dwight
D. Eisenhower.

Kefauver had really felt during the convention that he was
going to win. It was hard for him to accept the verdict of the
Louisville *Courier-Journal* that he, the "choice of the primaries and the rank and file, was repudiated because he exposed crime and graft in the administration."

If that was one reason for his repudiation, there was another which oddly paralleled it: Both were powerful factors
in his popularity as much as in his inability to take over
the Democratic party and the leadership of the nation.
William S. White, long-time Washington correspondent and
himself an ardent admirer of the Senate establishment (particularly its Southern wing) put it this way in his 1957 book
on the Senate entitled *Citadel:*

> The one unforgivable sin, the one exception to the
> policy of easy forgiveness, is to break with the clan upon a
> point of fundamentals. Senator Estes Kefauver of Tennes-
> see did this, in the Southern Senators' view, when early
> in his career it was represented that he opposed the fili-
> buster. He did it again when, in his "Crime Investiga-
> tion," in 1951 and 1952, he seemed to the Southerners to
> be undertaking to tell the states and municipalities what
> to do about their crime problems—and to be bathing in
> questionable publicity.
>
> For a time, by means as airy as a cloud but as cold as
> sleet, he was informally banished from the political com-
> pany of the Senate Southerners generally. This fact was
> one of the least known and most important circumstances
> of the 1952 Democratic Presidential convention.

Kefauver went there with impressive evidence of public support for the Democratic Presidential nomination. He never approached that nomination, in fact, and would not have, had the convention run three solid months instead of a week. The Southerners, though not in a position affirmatively to direct the convention, nevertheless had, with powerful allies from the North, quite enough power to block Kefauver. No other Southern purpose was so fixed, so implacable.

"To get along, go along," Sam Rayburn, Speaker of the House, used to tell every freshman class of Congressmen. "Rayburn's most illustrious protégé, President Lyndon Johnson," former Pennsylvania Senator Joseph Clark assures us, in his *Congress: The Sapless Branch,* "gave the same advice to newly elected Democratic Senators during his tenure as Majority Leader of the Senate."

Estes Kefauver had ignored the advice, and now at last the insiders of "the clan" had taken advantage of the opportunity to wreak vengeance. His colleague, Joseph Clark, was plagued by a growing conviction that the exclusive club to which the people of Pennsylvania had elected him was itself controlled by an inner core that was uninterested, in fact was adamantly opposed, to modernizing its own structure. In 1963, not too long before his own defeat for reelection, he delivered a historic speech (later published as *The Senate Establishment*) in which he attacked the bipartisan coalition as "a self-perpetuating oligarchy with mild, but only mild, overtones of plutocracy," that for a century or more has controlled the Senate and throttled Presidential programs.

This view paralleled that in Kefauver's own office. When his young counsel, Victor E. Ferrall, Jr., came to write a tribute to him in the *Yale Law Report,* he described the Senate club in these terms:

A good Senator plays a thoroughly institutionalized "game," with clearly defined rules. As a freshman he keeps out of mischief, does not make major floor speeches, and limits his energies to local matters. He may ask thoughtful, penetrating questions in his committee assignments, but he is retiring and definitely not a leader or spokesman of a particular position—even an approved position.

After a time—perhaps two years—he may tackle minor national issues. He is permitted, for example, to become an aspiring champion of heron conservation, anti-detergent pollution, or minor agricultural reforms. He may also deliver an occasional speech on major foreign or domestic policy, so long as he does not actively lead legislative actions.

To a very large extent, he must establish himself as a subservient and responsive follower of the Senate's established Senate leaders (vis-à-vis his administration leaders) well into his second term. In the process, of course, he also demonstrates his ability to be re-elected and, therefore, probable Senatorial longevity.

The Senate's memory is elephantine. If the aspiring Senator stumbles at any point along this long road of restraint, redemption is unlikely. Failure to play the "game" virtually assures exclusion from the club. Lack of club membership radically reduces effectiveness as a lawmaker.

Playing the "game" for ten or fifteen years, however, takes its toll. Surely so much calculated docility drains at least some of the conviction and vigor any Senator brings to the Congress as a freshman.

But Estes Kefauver had declined to be "docile," or "subservient," or "responsive," and in consequence he was faced with the unblinking, unyielding opposition of the establishment. Which way was there for him to turn? In a year he would be fifty. He loved the game of politics, the business of saying hello to thousands, patting women, hugging men, shaking all those hands, drinking with all those well-wishers, trying to be helpful; most of all he loved the idea that despite his basic shyness and remoteness he was doing what he was suited for, doing the public thing in order to be able to serve the public against those who would cheat and despoil it. But now, was there still a role for him to play?

eight ☆ Back to the Battle

☆☆☆ Candidate Stevenson, it developed that fall, was a witty and charming campaigner. Although he won only nine states against an obviously unbeatable man, he gained the affection of millions. He also won the respect, in some cases the adulation, of the intellectuals, who had been pretty much isolated from national affairs since the early days of the New Deal.

It was one of the minor ironies of Kefauver's career, already so studded with ironies, that the intellectuals would resist him—first in favor of Stevenson, finally in favor of John F. Kennedy. As Martha Ragland of Nashville, the long-time battler for human rights, puts it, Kefauver had been recognized as one of the nation's top Senators, "but once he began to threaten the establishment they began to label him as a buffoon."

Mrs. Ragland herself tended to regard him in the early days as an academic type, rather colorless, in fact. "He'd go further, I thought, if only he had flair."

When he demonstrated that flair, that magic touch with ordinary people, he was discarded, simply not taken seriously by the intellectuals. They did not see him as Martha Ragland did in 1953, after his defeat for the Presidential nomination, giving educational, "professorial" kinds of speeches to the people of Tennessee on economic and foreign policy. They did not hear him, as she did, driving to Nashville in her car and saying to her reflectively, "I think it was William James, with his moral equivalent for war, who posed the crucial problem for Tennesseeans." That was during the Korean conflict, in which Tennessee volunteers had once more hastened to participate. Mrs. Ragland has had occasion to rethink Kefauver's somber words during the agonizing Vietnam War, and the enthusiasm of so many of her neighbors for mindless militarism, for their sons' participation in that senseless destruction.

Although it had endeared him to Tennesseeans who liked to think of themselves as tough-minded and independent, unquestionably the coonskin cap damaged Kefauver nationally, particularly in the eyes of those who preferred to regard themselves as thoughtful, if not intellectual. Writing in *Harper's* magazine on the defeat of Kefauver's long-time colleague, Albert Gore, David Halberstam recalls Max Ascoli's sourly clever witticism about Kefauver: Many people, the magazine publisher once said, had succeeded in making themselves into highbrows; Kefauver may be the only highbrow who ever made himself into a lowbrow.

Mrs. Richard Borwick, a close family friend, traveled to Boston with the Senator in 1951 for a meeting at the Cambridge Faculty Club, and remembers how the cab driver who took them from the airport was more impressed with Kefauver the anticrime hero than were the professors with whom he met. It was one of the first occasions for a political figure to pick the brains of this group of academics, and there was a certain unease on both sides. For his part, he was trying to erase the country-bumpkin image. As for the professors, while they were somewhat impressed with his reputation as

A family grouping shows the young Estes Kefauver (at left) with his mother, Phredonia; his sister Nancy; and his brother, Robert.

At the University of Tennessee in 1922, Kefauver practiced hard
to make the football squad, where he played both guard and tackle.

Wide World Photos

The Kefauvers in 1952, when the Senator was making his first
Presidential bid: David, straddling his father's knee; Lynda,
holding the baby, Gail; and Diane, leaning against her mother.

As a young lawyer in
Chattanooga, Estes
Kefauver handled cases
of the underdogs—the
poor and the black.

On the campaign
circuit, Kefauver
sports his coonskin
cap, which had a
special meaning
for him, and also
for the people.

Both photos, Wide World Photos

(Above) The Crime Committee hearings were held in New York City's Federal courthouse in 1951. An electrifying parade of underworld figures appeared unwillingly to testify before Kefauver and his colleagues.

Candidate Kefauver pauses during the hectic Democratic National Convention in Chicago in 1952 to greet his father, Robert; his sister Nora; and his wife, Nancy (at right).

Senator Kefauver pledged his support to the 1954 Supreme Court desegregation ruling in Congress and in black communities. In San Francisco's Fillmore district and elsewhere he tried to show that a Southern drawl did not mean a prevailing Southern prejudice.

Wide World Photos

The Democratic team of Stevenson and Kefauver take off from Chicago in August of 1956 for a grass roots campaign.

Senator Kefauver and Dr. Frances Kelsey, of the Food and Drug
Administration, display a bottle of the dread drug thalidomide.
The 1962 scandal blew the lid off stalemated drug legislation.

a great reformer, it was apparent, as Mrs. Borwick puts it, that "he was not glib, nor had he mastered the semantics of the academic community."

Refreshed, if not made whole, after a rest in McMinnville, Tennessee, and a trip to Europe with Nancy, who was perhaps even more drained than he by the 1952 experience, Kefauver returned to Washington with an immediate project in mind.

Early in January of 1953 he introduced a constitutional amendment aimed at democratizing the American two-party system. Not only had he suffered bitterly from bossism—he was convinced that the American people had been cheated, not out of his candidacy as the indispensable man, but out of the right to have their own expressed preference taken into consideration.

His proposal was that state party primaries be written into the Constitution in order to give the people a clear voice in the selection of nominees. The matter was being discussed and studied not just in Washington but at the state level as well. But once again Kefauver was ahead of his time: In the wake of another Chicago debacle, this one in 1968, when hundreds of delegates and thousands of young people had worked furiously for Eugene McCarthy and Bobby Kennedy, only to see their rights and their aspirations trampled by cynical hacks, the cry for democratizing the "Party of the People" was once again to be raised. But in the wake of Stevenson's brave (if foredoomed) campaign, and the euphoria of the new Eisenhower administration, Kefauver's proposed amendment was pushed aside and forgotten.

The temper of the times was such that liberals were being forced onto the defensive. Far from being able to muster extensive support for social-reform programs, they found themselves fighting rearguard actions to keep existing social measures and civil liberties intact. These were the years when Joe McCarthy was riding high. Terrorizing government employees and private citizens alike with his wild, free-swinging, unanswerable charges, he succeeded in infecting both the ambitious and the frightened with his particular brand of venom.

Kefauver had made it perfectly clear where he stood by remaining firm over the years—fighting the Federal Employment Loyalty Act, opposing permanent status for the House Un-American Activities Committee, voting against both the McCarran Immigration Act and the Internal Security Act of 1950. Now he was opposed for renomination to the Senate in the 1954 primary by a Congressman who figured it would be shrewd to beat him with two clubs—his refusal to condemn the historic Supreme Court decision outlawing racial segregation in the nation's schools, and his refusal to play the popular game of hunting down "Reds."

Kefauver struck back on both issues. "There is not one thing that a member of the United States Senate can do about that decision," he said of the Supreme Court decision, "and anyone who tells you that he's going to do something about it is just trying to mislead you for votes."

On the "Red" issue, he spoke up in defense of his friends who were being attacked as "known Communists," and attacked politicians who attempted to gain political advantage by "calling a citizen a 'known Communist' one day and then apologizing in a wee, small voice the next."

The primary campaign of Kefauver's opponent was not only dirty, but well-financed by right-wing fringe groups and Texas oil money. Through these financial resources his opposition was able to reach remote rural areas by helicopter and to blanket the state with TV talkathons, twelve- to twenty-four-hour programs in which libelous accusations were made against him. Accused of everything from being uninterested in Tennessee to being soft on Communists, Kefauver stuck to the issues and refused to backtrack.

Sitting in his room in Nashville, Richard Wallace, the Memphis journalist who had become Kefauver's administrative assistant in 1951, was not too surprised to have Ed Orgill walk in and say, "Dick, we're in terrible shape. We need help badly." Orgill rang up Elmo Roper in New York and expressed his fear that without the wherewithal to reach the people and enable Kefauver to be heard, the prospect was bleak.

By luck Roper ran into Averell Harriman, one of the wealthiest men in the Democratic party. Harriman heard Roper out and then, with some reluctance—he is not noted for his openhandedness—wrote a check for the Kefauver campaign in the amount of a thousand dollars.

But when primary day was over, Kefauver had not merely squeaked through. He had won by a whopping 3-to-1 margin, taking all but 4 of the state's 95 counties. When Harriman heard the news, he inquired somewhat dourly of Elmo Roper, "Say, how much margin do you allow when you take a poll?"

The general election still lay ahead, however, and in Washington frightened liberals were coming to the conclusion that the politic thing to do would be to out-McCarthy Senator McCarthy.

"The vote that most impressed me," Clarence Streit has written, "allowed one to test Estes against the whole field. It came when 'northern Democratic liberals,' with whom Estes often voted, sought during the McCarthy fever to outfox those who charged that they were soft on Communism, by sponsoring a bill to outlaw the Communist party." This bill, known as the Humphrey amendment to outlaw membership in the Communist party, has been described by Douglass Cater as "a rather cute effort by Senate liberals to outdo the right-wing vigilantes."

Kefauver's response to Hubert Humphrey's "cute effort" has been well recorded by Richard Wallace:

> Although the Senator was successful in the primary, it was still uncertain, on that August afternoon, who his Republican opponent would be in November. The Tennessee papers were full of speculation that it would be Ray Jenkins, who had served as counsel in the Army-McCarthy hearings. . . .
>
> Furthermore, the Senator's supporters were still gun-shy of the "soft on Communism" charge after their summer of it. . . .
>
> In the House, a group of Republican Congressmen, looking forward to the fall elections, filed an anti-Communist bill, largely meaningless, and it passed. The bill came to the Senate, where a group of Democratic members, also looking forward to the fall elections, decided that they would prove, once and for all, that the Democrats were more anti-Communist than the Republicans. An amendment was proposed to the bill which would have made it a crime to belong to the Communist party.
>
> . . . instinctively, he didn't like that amendment. He said so. He asked his staff to research the law and determine what its actual effect would be, but things were moving so fast that it wasn't possible to complete the research until after the final vote had been taken.
>
> Estes, however, argued extemporaneously against it.

The *Congressional Record* of August 17, 1954, gives a bit of the flavor of that argument:

SEN. KEFAUVER: Many of us are concerned about the precedent of outlawing a particular group. Perhaps next year Congress will not like some other group. In the history of this Nation, is this a new approach to the problem? Have we ever outlawed any group before in the history of the United States? In the history of our Nation, has any group ever been outlawed or condemned as illegal by legislative enactment?

SEN. HUMPHREY: Let me say to my friend, the senior Senator from Tennessee, that we are not outlawing now the Women's League, the Democrats, the Republicans. . . .

Mr. Wallace continues his account:

He was under considerable pressure from back home to cease his opposition. Moreover, the Democratic leadership on the Senate floor advised him to be silent as he was hurting the "liberal image" of a number of Senators who were backing or sponsoring the amendment. Senator Kefauver's answer was: "I can't. It's a bad bill. I've got to oppose it." . . .

Estes Kefauver and I walked off the floor together and back to the office. When we got there, the telephones were ringing from Tennessee. I took a call from one of his staunchest supporters in Memphis, one who had stuck his neck out six years earlier to stand with Estes when to do so was to incur the wrath of Boss Crump.

"Dick," he said, "we've been watching the progress of that fight up there in the Senate and a group of us have decided that the best way for Estes to scotch that 'soft on

Communism' charge is for him to get in there and support the bill."

"You're a little late," I said. "They just voted."

"What was the vote?" came the question that I knew would come.

"Eighty-one to one," I answered.

"And how did Estes vote?" he asked, in somewhat shocked dismay.

"Estes was the one," I answered.

He exploded: "How the hell do you and Estes expect us to explain that eighty-one members of the Senate were wrong and he was right?"

Nonetheless, when Wallace phoned Lucius Burch and asked him to try to explain Kefauver's position to the people in Tennessee, Burch replied, "The local people are saying, 'What convictions the man has!' "

They were not the only ones who were having second thoughts. The very day after he had voted his conscience, quite alone, two of his most distinguished colleagues, Paul Douglas and Herbert Lehman, took the floor to confess that their consciences had not allowed them to sleep all night, because they too should have voted as Kefauver had. Mrs. Richard Borwick recalls vividly not only how Estes had said to her before the vote, "I'm getting an awful lot of mail from my constituency on it," but how two days after the vote Senator Wayne Morse of Oregon said simply to Nancy Kefauver, "Lady, your husband has guts."

For once his courage had a quick impact. The bill, conceived in hysteria and voted up in cowardice, was quietly pigeonholed as one of dubious constitutionality. And when Joe McCarthy threatened to attack him in his usual fashion if Kefauver were to dare accept an anti-McCarthy speaking engagement in Wisconsin, Kefauver had the satisfaction not only of fulfilling the engagement, but of winning re-election in November with ease.

During this period, the powerful private utility corporations had set to work once again to undermine TVA, which not only produced all the electric power consumed in Tennessee and elsewhere, but had become a way of life to the people of the area. Encouraged by the election of the first Republican President in twenty years, and his selection of a Cabinet consisting of "nine millionaires and a plumber," the private utilities had no difficulty in persuading Dwight Eisenhower that TVA ought to be cut back as a lesson to "creeping Socialism."

Eisenhower's first budget, therefore, omitted funds for a new steam plant that TVA needed in order to provide power for the atomic plants at Oak Ridge, Tennessee, and Paducah, Kentucky. Instead, a study of steam plant needs was made by the Bureau of the Budget, which did determine that, just as TVA had estimated, there was indeed a power shortage of 600,000 kilowatts. When it came to deciding what to do about it, though, the Budget Bureau turned not to TVA, but to an unpaid consultant named Adolph Wenzell.

Wenzell, who had come to the Bureau in the spring of 1954, was a vice president of the First Boston Corporation, a private financing outfit serving utilities. So it was hardly surprising that in the fall of 1954 Wenzell recommended an end to TVA expansion. He went even further: He proposed that TVA's power system (with the exception of its multipurpose dams) be handed over to the private utilities.

Meanwhile, Gordon Clapp, Chairman of TVA, had been turned down by the Budget Bureau in his request for a new

TVA steam plant at Fulton Landing, on the banks of the Mississippi. He suggested next that the Atomic Energy Commission, which had become TVA's biggest customer, obtain its power supply elsewhere, and allow TVA to use its output for other needs.

The Budget Bureau accepted Clapp's suggestion, and instructed the AEC (which had been buying power from both a TVA plant and a private power plant) to look for another supplier. Now, however, came some fancy finagling, which was to outrage the people of the Tennessee Valley and catapult Kefauver to the center of the stage once again.

The AEC worked out a deal with the Budget Bureau whereby the commission would contract for power, not just for itself, but for TVA as well. Instead of the originally proposed TVA power plant outside of Memphis, a plant would be built there by private industry, which would sell power to AEC—which would in turn distribute it to TVA.

Edgar Dixon and Eugene Yates were the principals in an electrical combine that agreed to take on the private end of the job in this complex operation, if they could get financing. Unknown to the public, Adolph Wenzell, who had left Washington after his initial attack on TVA, was quietly called back to the capital once again to work on financing the Dixon-Yates deal.

Even though they were not yet aware of the role being played by the shadowy Wenzell, supporters of TVA were indignant. If Dixon-Yates went through, TVA would be forced to take power from private corporations at higher rates than it would have cost from its own proposed plant. And since the AEC had no legal right to sign a long-term contract, President Eisenhower was proposing an amendment to the Atomic Energy Act to legalize the proposed deal.

Kefauver was caught up in his campaign for re-election (which at the time looked dubious), and had to content himself for the moment with issuing public statements of this order: "AEC is being used by order of President Eisenhower and with the active encouragement of the Budget Bureau for no other purposes than to act as a power broker for a reluctant TVA." In his eyes, the Dixon-Yates deal was "about the same as directing the U.S. Wild Life Service to run a brewery." He observed:

> The contract paves the way for the most unworkable administrative operation that anyone in Washington has yet been able to dream up. And the shame of it is that it is designed to wreck the most efficient of all government operations, the Tennessee Valley Authority, an innocent bystander. If the Dixon-Yates deal goes through, a lot of municipal and rural cooperatives are in for devouring, and the consumers all over the nation will feel the digestive pains.

Brave words, but it seemed certain nonetheless that Dixon-Yates was going to be put over on the unsuspecting American consuming public. Kefauver's Tennessee colleague, Senator Albert Gore, led a very tough struggle, but in the end was unable to prevent the AEC, on orders from the President of the United States, from signing the Dixon-Yates contract.

The President, however, had been stung by the charges that he was not really aware of what was going on, and was overly responsive to pressure from his businessmen friends; he directed the AEC to make public the history of the events leading up to the signing of the contract. From the point of view of the behind-the-scenes operators, it was the worst thing that could have happened—next to Kefauver's winning his re-election campaign and returning to Washington eager to expose the deal.

In a last-ditch effort to get rid of the Dixon-Yates contract, the municipal and cooperative power systems of the State of Tennessee, thirty-seven in all, hired a lawyer named Joe Volpe. Going through subpoenaed papers of the Securities and Exchange Commission, Volpe came upon the name of Adolph Wenzell. What did it mean? He went to the Budget Bureau, which insisted that Wenzell was not and never had been a paid employee of the Bureau—but then refused to elaborate. What did that mean?

At about this point Kefauver was freed to enter the picture. As it happened, he enjoyed excellent relations with Bill Langer, the maverick North Dakota Senator who ran (in the Republican-organized Senate) the Judiciary Committee. Far from being a hard-line party man, Langer was himself a Populist of sorts who, as Richard Wallace recollects, said frankly to Kefauver, "I'm going to look to you to help run the Antitrust Subcommittee."

Kefauver got the liberal lawyer Sidney Davis to come down from New York City to run a subcommittee furnished with neither staff nor money. Together with Wallace, they pursued the Dixon-Yates investigation "on a shoestring," as Wallace puts it.

Kefauver set to work to get the story of Wenzell's wire-pulling out into the open, despite President Eisenhower's assertion that "Mr. Wenzell was never called in or asked a single thing about the Dixon-Yates contract." Kefauver suspected, with some justification, that the President was not fully aware of what was being done in his name, and said as

much publicly. In consequence Mr. Eisenhower announced
that the Dixon-Yates contract would be reviewed, and the
role of Wenzell examined.

But now Kefauver and his small band were hot on the
trail. Roland Hughes, Director of the Budget Bureau, was
followed to the subcommittee witness stand by Chairman
J. Sinclair Armstrong of the Securities and Exchange Commission. Armstrong refused to respond to Kefauver's questions on Adolph Wenzell, invoking executive privilege. It
was a matter on which he did not have the legal right to
claim such privilege, and Kefauver quietly suggested that
Armstrong go back to Attorney General Herbert Brownell
and talk it over with him.

This happened over and over, with Armstrong taking the
stand and refusing to testify. Finally, faced with the evidence, and with Kefauver's insistence that he had a legal
obligation to reply, Armstrong admitted that Sherman
Adams, the Presidential assistant, had been responsible for
blocking the public hearings which would have exposed
Wenzell's role in the whole scheme.

President Eisenhower, noting that the City of Memphis
had taken matters into its own hands and voted to build its
own steam plant, took advantage of the development to de-
clare the Dixon-Yates contract cancelled.

It was a triumph not just for TVA or for Tennessee, but
for the people. Kefauver saw the investigation through to
the finish, revealing to the public how Wenzell had set up
the basic scheme for Dixon-Yates and served as the financier
whose First Boston Corporation would be backing the
scheme to make the public pay more for its power. Dixon
and Yates were finished, and TVA was saved from being
chewed to pieces—and just at the moment when most liberals

were asserting that nothing could be done to protect it from the attacks of private interests that were emboldened by friends in the White House.

With Congress in summer recess following the Dixon-Yates exposé, Kefauver took off in the latter part of 1955 for a trip around the world. It was neither a handshaking expedition nor a summer vacation, but a means of getting personal perspective on the big problems he had first tackled back in the 1940's with his public espousal of Atlantic Union.

The trip took him to seventeen countries, and included visits to Eastern Europe, the Soviet Union, the Middle East, and the Far East. In the course of these visits he had the opportunity—denied to the typical tourist, but available to the Presidential candidate who may one day become the most important single statesman in the world—to sit down and talk with world leaders.

And so Kefauver relaxed his big frame in a series of informal conversations with Bulganin and Khrushchev in Moscow, Rakosi in Budapest, Tito in Belgrade, Chamoun in Lebanon, Nehru in New Delhi, Syngman Rhee in Seoul, Diem in Saigon, Abdul Rahman in Malaya. (Earlier in the year, when, as Douglass Cater reports, "the Formosa Strait resolution was being whipped through Congress with alarmist shouts, Kefauver . . . submitted an amendment of his own removing the risky offshore provisions. . . . Unlike a number of his colleagues who backed and filled during this panicky period, he maintained a steady course." He was, veteran Washington observer I. F. Stone concurs, "one of the few who tried to keep the doors open in the Far East for a United Nations settlement of the dispute over both Formosa and the offshore islands.")

By the time he got back home Kefauver felt that he was

ready to present himself to the voters once again as a Presidential candidate in the 1956 campaign. And once again he had an opportunity to make his peace with the Senate's Southern bloc. No doubt it was already much too late for that, but most politicians with national ambitions would have grasped the opportunity (indeed, Adlai Stevenson made a point of journeying to Alabama to assure white Southerners that he was understanding of their "problems") .

All of the Senators from below the Mason-Dixon line banded together to issue what they ringingly entitled the Southern Manifesto. Quite simply, it was a statement of refusal to abide by the law of the land, as enunciated in the historic Supreme Court decision of 1954 on school desegregation.

Many have underestimated the local pressures on Estes Kefauver to go along with the Southern bloc. Noting that Tennessee is a border state and that, as one which had been (particularly in the east) pro-Union, it was the first Southern state to be readmitted to the Union after the Civil War, they see Kefauver's refusal to use the traditional Southern political ploy of yelling "nigger" as a comparatively easy liberalism. A glance through the endless folders of his mail in the Kefauver wing of the University of Tennessee Library suffices to dispel this illusion.

It was not just the red-necks who scrawled messages of race hatred to their senior Senator. On July 4, 1957, a constituent who was himself a lawyer warned Kefauver of the consequence if he did not oppose a pending civil rights bill: "The TVA is a minor matter compared with this matter; we can live without electricity, but not with integration. Be sure to represent the people who elected you."

Knowing all this far better than the Northern liberals who

could still view "this matter" from a safe distance, Kefauver
yet did not hesitate. He refused to sign the Southern Manifesto, and thereby ensured what he must have known would
result. The Southerners, as William S. White wrote in
Citadel, "in 1956 fought his nomination for Vice President
as long as they could stand and fight."

But Kefauver gained something which must have been at
least as important to him—the respect and affection of countless Negroes, ironic in that Negro leaders recognized how
public praise could only hurt him politically with the racists.
The following letter, on the stationery of the Washington
bureau of the National Association for the Advancement of
Colored People, was headed PERSONAL. It is here made public for what is no doubt the first time.

April 5, 1956

Honorable Estes Kefauver
Senate Office Building
Washington, D.C.

Dear Estes:

Because this is a campaign year and the NAACP is non-
partisan, I am sending you this personal letter. In politics,
I am an Independent and I obey our organization's requirement not to endorse any candidate for public office.
The simple purpose I have in mind at this time is to
thank you for your Florida statement that the U.S.
Supreme Court was exercising its constitutional authority
when it ruled on the school segregation cases.

No one can tell what the years ahead hold for our country,
but, along with you, I believe that our future is full of

promise for all of our people—North and South. I, too, believe that we are one people, whether we live in Mississippi or Massachusetts—whether we be white or black.

Even before the Supreme Court decision, I firmly believed that the South would repudiate racial segregation. That belief is strengthened now. I also believe that when men who seek public office face up to realities, as you have in this case, thousands of citizens will be encouraged to speak out for what is right.

No doubt you will take positions on other matters with which I shall disagree. But I could not let this moment pass without letting you know what is in my heart.

Cordially yours,
Clarence

Clarence Mitchell
Director
Washington Bureau

"We had a feeling during his last years," Martha Ragland reflects, "that Estes tended to make our State more liberal. He had a sheltering umbrella over the rest of us."

The faithful Harry Mansfield, looking back on the years since Kefauver's death, feels that "it was Kefauver who was responsible for Tennessee's not having any more social unrest than we did" during the eruptions of the 1960's. "He was the exact opposite of a rabble-rouser. He had a leavening effect."

In 1956 Kefauver decided once more to go the exhausting primary route to the Democratic party convention. He was directly challenging Adlai Stevenson's bid for renomination, and indeed Kefauver won the primaries in Wisconsin, in

Minnesota, in Maryland. But now he was opposed, even if with reluctance and sadness, by some who had been his closest allies—loyal friends like Paul Douglas who felt that Stevenson had demonstrated his leadership and was entitled to another go. In the more crucial primaries of California, Oregon, and Florida, Kefauver was swamped, and he went to the Chicago convention aware that this time his hopes were minimal.

He felt, however—as did countless others—that he was entitled to second place on the national ticket. Stevenson himself, rather than exercise the Presidential nominee's traditional option of selecting his own running mate, declared that he would be happy to run with the man the delegates would select. It seemed fairly clear that that man would be Estes Kefauver.

But matters were not that simple. As Elmo Roper recalled, Tennessee Governor Sid McMath returned to the Kefauver camp from a scouting expedition to Stevenson headquarters crying angrily: "Let's go home, it's not an open convention. Stevenson has already given the Vice Presidential nomination to Jack Kennedy." Roper continued:

> Wilson Wyatt, my closest friend, was Adlai's campaign manager. He said, "Between you and me, Adlai leans to Estes rather than to Jack. In fact, it would be nice if the two sat down and had a talk."
>
> So I went from the Blackstone to the Stevens, where I saw Nancy Kefauver. She said, "You'd better go on in there—they're trying to get Estes to go home." Inside, I found Dick Wallace quietly trying to get Estes to stay, and I added my voice to his. I told Estes what I knew, and urged that he not go home, but stay—despite the fact that Sid McMath was furious—for a talk with Adlai.

He did just that, and emerged after about twenty minutes to tell me that he was convinced that Adlai was on the level about its being an open convention, and that he was now determined to stay on and fight for the Vice Presidential nomination.

It became clear very quickly that the contest was to be between Estes Kefauver and the young Senator from Massachusetts, the ambitious and (thanks in part to the family fortune) extremely well-organized campaigner, John F. Kennedy. At the point during the maneuverings when it seemed as if the two men might be deadlocked, Kefauver's younger Tennessee colleague, Albert Gore, decided that he might utilize his control of the Tennessee delegation to present himself as an alternative choice.

Gore's ambitious move infuriated a number of men in the Tennessee camp. Silliman Evans, Jr., who had succeeded to the management of the Nashville *Tennesseean* upon the death of his father, leaped to his feet in a rage. (It was the senior Evans who had said to Kefauver back in 1948: "If you promise to shake five hundred hands a day between now and Election Day, I'll back you.") The younger Evans was a short pudgy man. He reached up to grab Senator Gore's lapels and swore: "If you don't release the Tennessee delegation to Kefauver, I'll blast you in my paper. You won't get elected dogcatcher, much less Senator!" Then Evans took out his watch and added, "You've got two minutes to get out of the race."

Albert Gore got the message, Estes Kefauver got the nomination, and he embarked with Adlai Stevenson upon a desperate and hopeless effort—trying to turn Dwight Eisenhower out of the White House.

In the midst of their uphill drive, two events of enormous

international significance—the Russian tank assault on the
rebellious people of Budapest, and the Anglo-French invasion of Suez—aroused world tensions and solidified the
American people more firmly than ever behind their Gen-
eral-President. After Suez, the Stevenson-Kefauver campaign
was doomed.

Once more Kefauver's struggle was to have ironic overtones. He had bested Jack Kennedy—and thereby had succeeded in consigning himself to an impossible effort and in
keeping alive Kennedy's political future. The lesson was not
lost on John F. Kennedy, as he later revealed in an interview with columnist Bob Considine.

Asked about his brother, Joe, the oldest of the Kennedy
boys, who had been killed in World War II, Jack Kennedy
replied:

"I'll tell you about Joe. He was the star among the kids.
He was taller than the rest of us, stronger, better-looking.
He was the best athlete of the bunch, could jump higher,
run faster, hit harder. He brought home the best report
cards.

"Joe would have been the politician of the family, not
me. Joe would have won the Congressional seat from our
district in 1946. Joe would have beaten Henry Cabot
Lodge for his Senate seat in 1952. Joe would have beaten
Estes Kefauver last Summer for the Vice Presidential
nomination, where I just missed. It would have been a
Stevenson-Kennedy ticket."

He paused and grinned.

"And Eisenhower would have knocked his brains out.
Right now, Joe would be picking up the broken pieces of
his political career."

The young Senator paused again.

"I guess I owe a lot to Estes," he said reflectively.

Kefauver himself was under no illusions as to the outcome of the campaign. Sitting in a suite with Charles Tyroler and Harry Mansfield, he said flatly, "Suez will cost us the election—the only thing we can do is salvage as much as we can."

By salvaging, Kefauver meant saving as many Congressional seats as possible for his fellow Democrats. The Democratic strategy, which Kefauver accepted completely, was for Stevenson to make the high-level policy speeches, while his running mate did the drudgery, making countless appearances at the side of office-seekers across the country.

The fact that he was not going to win did not mean to Kefauver that he could let up in his effort to save what could be saved. Just the opposite. He turned it into a killing job, driving himself like a man possessed. Jowanda Shelton, who joined his staff that year, made every trip with him. Much of it is now a blur. "When it was all over I slept for three days in a row."

"He wore the hell out of us on that campaign," says Richard Wallace. "We covered thirty-eight states in eight weeks. It was 85,000 miles worth of checking into a hotel at 3 A.M. and checking out at 6 A.M."

Kefauver's entire strategy was designed to bait Richard Nixon, his opponent in the Vice Presidential race, into fighting back. The Kefauvers and the Nixons had lived one block from each other in Spring Valley, Maryland, the Kefauver children and the Nixon girls had attended the same neighborhood elementary school, but two more different men could not be imagined.

The research division of the Democratic National Committee got up a fact sheet on the Congressional voting records of the two candidates. The comparison was based on votes taken while both were serving in the House (1947 and 1948) and in the Senate (1951 and 1952), and on comparable House and Senate votes during 1949 and 1950, when Kefauver was in the Senate and Nixon still in the House. In every one of the dozen areas selected, the contrast was devastating.

In agriculture, Nixon had voted for cuts in the soil-conservation program and the farm-information program, and Kefauver against. Kefauver had voted for continuing the farm tenant-loan program, Nixon against. In the field of business, Nixon had voted to exempt natural-gas producers from Federal price regulation, and for weakening the anti-trust laws; Kefauver had voted against. In health, education, and welfare Nixon had voted against the "oil for education" amendment (which would provide that revenue from Federal operation of submerged lands should be devoted to Federal aid to education during nonemergency times), and Kefauver for; Nixon had voted to cut funds for schools in areas overcrowded because of defense activity or government installations, and Kefauver against; Nixon had voted against increasing school lunch funds and strengthening the aid-to-medical-schools program, and Kefauver had voted for.

On TVA and public power, the records of the two men were again diametrically opposed. So too in votes on public housing, middle-income housing, labor, public works, rural electrification, Social Security, offshore oil, income taxes, capital gains tax, corporation income tax, and on the Point Four and foreign aid programs, as well as on immigration and displaced persons bills.

Kefauver hammered so unmercifully at Richard Nixon

on the issues that the Vice President had to be forcibly re-strained from fighting back. But the Republican strategy was simplicity itself—a vote of confidence in Ike, the kindly father figure—and issues were to be avoided like the plague.

People were tired from World War II and Korea and the exhausting business of catching up on those lost years; they were frightened by ominous international developments. And they were all too willing to trust Ike while they concentrated on making a living and a little better life for their children.

Kefauver had chosen the wrong decade in which to appeal to the consciences and the minds of the American people. Or so it seemed. And in 1957, even though the Gallup Poll still showed him the most popular political figure, and the newspapers still ran headlines like: SEN. KEFAUVER TOPS DEMOCRATS IN NEWEST TEST, *Kennedy, Johnson, and Clement Run Second, Third, and Fourth,* it was clear that Estes Kefauver was finished. At fifty-three, as far as national significance and the power to affect events were concerned, he seemed to be through.

But he was not. He was standing on the threshold of his finest achievements.

nine ☆ The Great Years

☆☆☆ During the year before he made his Vice Presidential run, Kefauver had chaired a subcommittee that wrote
a kind of postscript to his crime inquiry. Its reports on
"Comic Books and Juvenile Delinquency" and on "Television and Juvenile Delinquency" had been unexception-
able in tone and conclusions: ". . . neither the comic book
industry nor any other sector of the media of mass communications can absolve itself from responsibility for the effects
of its product. Attempts to shift all responsibility to parents
are unjustified . . . this country cannot afford the calculated risk of feeding its children, through comic books, a
concentrated diet of crime, horror, and violence."

And on the television industry: "The generally violent
mood in which our society dwells must be counteracted with
a more positive, relaxed environment for the child to grow
in. Of course the ultimate responsibility for such an atmosphere rests with the parents. But another place to break
the vicious cycle of constant stimuli of violence is in the
communications media. During the years that the child looks
at television he forms the whole set of firmly held convictions about the world with which he will meet adulthood."

The way in which the first generation reared on horror
comics and television violence met adulthood became in-

118

creasingly clear in the assassinations and racial clashes that
marked the 1960's. Viewed in this light the Kefauver reports can be seen as prophetic.

But perhaps even more significant was his subcommittee
report's emphasis on the near-monopolistic control of the
comic book industry:

> On first impression, the present comic book industry
> would seem to comprise many different publishing firms
> with no apparent relationship of one to another. On
> closer scrutiny, however, it is found that the picture is en-
> tirely different.
>
> Information obtained by the subcommittee indicates
> that, while there are 112 seemingly separate and distinct
> corporations engaged in the publication of comic books,
> these corporations, through such devices as common
> stockholders and officer and family ties, are in actual fact
> owned and controlled by a relatively small group of men
> and women.

Kefauver was determined not to allow exploiters of the
people (including those whose acts had not yet been defined
as criminal) escape from their responsibility by claiming
that they were merely part of a broadly owned series of operations responding to a broad series of public needs. This was
to become the consuming passion of Kefauver's last six years.

With the reorganization of the Congress in 1957, Kefauver took over the chairmanship of the Senate Judiciary
Committee's Subcommittee on Antitrust and Monopoly.
Now he had the authority to proceed with the investigation
of a whole network of abuses to which the American people
were being subjected; and he hastened to take advantage of

the opportunity, building a staff which, for intellectual probity and dedication, was to prove the envy of his colleagues.

The cutting edge of Kefauver's cross-examining thrust was to become apparent even before his subcommittee was in full swing. A joint hearing, called "Emergency Oil Lift Program and Related Oil Problems," was held before the subcommittee of the Committee on the Judiciary and the Committee on Interior and Insular Affairs of the 85th Congress. It would be beyond our scope to go into the complexities of that investigation of a supposed oil shortage resulting from the Suez crisis. Those complexities have been unraveled by Robert Engler in his *The Politics of Oil,* which concludes that on the entire matter of presumed shortage and possible rationing "the American government's position was vague and evasive."

President Eisenhower's Assistant Secretary of the Interior, Felix E. Wormser, was subjected to an examination by Senator Kefauver which should have given the captains of industry a foretaste of what lay ahead for them:

SEN. KEFAUVER: Isn't it true that the big companies don't want the independents to increase their crude [oil] production and that you have done nothing substantially about it, yourself?

MR. WORMSER: I have never had a company express that thought to me, sir. . . .

SEN. KEFAUVER: Isn't it true that the big companies on your committee fix the international rate for the price of oil on the world market?

MR. WORMSER: I don't know, sir. . . .

SEN. KEFAUVER: What justification do you find for the domestic increase in the price of oil by Humble Oil, followed by many of the others?

MR. WORMSER: I should respectfully suggest that you direct that to the Humble Oil Company. . . .

SEN. KEFAUVER: Might you not even make an effort to protect the American consumer?

MR. WORMSER: Not on prices, sir. We are leaving that severely alone, unless it is specifically directed by Congress. . . .

SEN. KEFAUVER: Do you contemplate asking Congress to do anything on prices?

MR. WORMSER: No, sir.

SEN. KEFAUVER: You mean you are going to sit by and let these companies raise prices?

MR. WORMSER: Operating under a free enterprise economy, sir, I would expect that a free enterprise will take care of it. . . .

SEN. KEFAUVER: Nobody can prevent you from asking these companies to be decent, and hold the prices down. What prevents you from doing so?

MR. WORMSER: Well, I think that is foreign to our responsibility, sir . . . it would be an interference with the free market. . . .

SEN. KEFAUVER: In the face of the President's general expression of interest and his request, you are going to do nothing to try to keep these prices down?

MR. WORMSER: No, sir. . . .

SEN. KEFAUVER: That is an encouragement for these big companies, because that certainly would be an invitation for other Humble Oil operations, which would set up a chain reaction.

MR. WORMSER: We could make an appeal like the President

has, but apparently the people of the United States have heard that appeal. . . . We could repeat the President's appeal to the public. I suppose we can do that. I have no objection to that. . . .

SEN. KEFAUVER: Do you have any idea how much additional profits these companies have made by reason of this voluntary agreement?

MR. WORMSER: None whatsoever. . . . We have nothing to do, sir, with the profits of any of the oil companies. . . . These companies are acting at the Government's request. . . .

SEN. KEFAUVER: Suppose they raise the price ten cents a gallon. Would you do anything about that?

MR. WORMSER: Nothing at all. . . .

SEN. KEFAUVER: Fifty cents a gallon?

MR. WORMSER: It is entirely up to them whether they raise it. . . . As a matter of fact, Senator, so far as I am concerned . . . I haven't declared myself for or against a price increase. I am completely neutral, sir.

In its first foray into the American corporate jungle Kefauver's Antitrust and Monopoly Subcommittee went directly to the lair of the largest of all the beasts—steel. Kefauver wrote in his posthumously published book on monopoly, *In a Few Hands*:

The average consumer never thinks of buying a pound of steel, yet the steel industry's role in our economy is fundamental. Our machine economy, with its heavy dependence upon steel, makes us peculiarly vulnerable to the pricing decisions in the steel industry. If the price of steel goes up, the inflationary impact is felt throughout the entire economic structure . . . it is not surprising that a $6 a ton increase in the price of steel, according to one expert, results in a $75 increase in the price of a tractor; nor that a $25 increase in sheet-steel prices ultimately means an increase to the purchaser of an automobile of over $50.

Between the end of World War II and the onset of the Kefauver inquiry, the steel industry had boosted its prices twelve separate times, at incalculable cost to the American people. Why? And why didn't there seem to be anything that anyone could do about it, beyond Kefauver's repeated warnings to President Eisenhower and the latter's appeal to the steel manufacturers—and the United Steelworkers—to "exercise restraint"?

One of the key facts that Kefauver brought out in the steel-price hearings in the summer and fall of 1957 was that the industry was playing the game of follow-the-leader. He was patient, he was painstaking, he was unfailingly courteous in allowing the industry executives to ramble on with endless answers to his probing questions. But it became clear, as he reported in his subsequent book, that

As the officials of the leading corporations in an industry parade through a Congressional hearing room, they often seem to have been constructed from the same mold. Sometimes this similarity is not confined to the rather uniform way they view the industry's problems and defend its set of trade practices. On occasion it extends to general physical appearance, pattern of dress, and even sense of humor, which becomes manifest at one time or another during the hearings.

The rationale for an industry's price structure follows

rather set patterns. In drugs, the magic word is "research." In automobiles, it is "the public's insistent demand" for style changes. In steel, it is "high labor costs." In each of these industries, something sacrosanct has become attached to these particular concepts, and there is little disposition to subject them to critical examination.

It was precisely Kefauver's determination to examine these sacred cows that made him such a threat to those committed to milking not the cows but the consumer. He saw no reason to take it for granted that the steelworkers were the culprits in the never-ending cycle of steel-price rises and painful inflation simply because this was the manufacturers' explanation.

In steel the defense for high prices centers around the level of steel wages as compared with those in other industries [Kefauver wrote]. The unit of measurement preferred by the industry is cost "per employee-hour." Now, if the steel industry were selling man-hours of work, as happens in a law office or in a firm of consulting engineers, that would be one thing. But, as everyone knows, the industry is engaged in the marketing of steel and steel products. The incidence of technological progress is constantly to lower man-hour requirements in production; according to a variety of estimates, the average annual rate of increase in man-hour productivity in the steel industry is between 3 and 4 per cent. As a result, employment costs per ton of steel shipped may decline or hold even, while employment costs "per employee-hour" rise. This simple fact was pointed out again and again during

the subcommittee's hearings in 1957. Yet "cost per employee-hour" was used as justification for higher prices by
the industry in 1962 and again in 1963.

As Kefauver observed, the follow-the-leader game might
make sense to an outsider if the price movement were down-
ward, and one company tried to compete with a rival by
lowering its prices. But how could you make sense of it
when, after a major steel company raised its prices, the
others "competed" by *raising* their prices to the exact same
point?

The answer, as Kefauver developed it in the hearings, was
roughly that this was not "free enterprise," and that steel
prices were not "competitive" but *administered*—a concept
originally developed by the economist Gardiner C. Means to
indicate that prices were arrived at not in response to the
laws of supply and demand, but by private decision of the
steel executives as to just how much the market would bear.
What follows, as Means put it in his book, *Pricing Power
and the Public Interest,* is "the tendency of different companies producing a standard product to set identical prices
for the same product."

Means quotes the following revealing testimony of Roger
N. Blough, then Chairman of the Board of U.S. Steel:

MR. BLOUGH: If we offer to sell steel at the same price as a
competitor at the customer's door, that is very definitely
a competitive price with our customer. Now, it isn't a
different price and, therefore, it isn't a noncompetitive
price, but it is a competitive price.
SEN. KEFAUVER: You mean it will give him the right to decide whether he will buy his steel from you or Bethlehem

Steel? That is the only difference, isn't it? That is the only competition? If you offer to sell a customer at the same price as Bethlehem, the only point of competition is whether they buy from you or whether they buy from Bethlehem, isn't it, or some other company?

MR. BLOUGH: That certainly isn't the only point of competition. There are many elements.

SEN. KEFAUVER: What is the other point where you offer the same price?

MR. BLOUGH: Well, you have quality, you have service, and you have many other aspects of competition, which are all very important elements. . . .

SEN. KEFAUVER: Mr. Blough, do you regard it as true competition when another company matches your price to a thousandth of a cent per pound, or you match some other company's price to a thousandth of a cent per pound? Wouldn't it be more competitive if there were at least some slight difference in these prices?

I mean, what difference does it make who they buy from if the prices are going to be identical to one-thousandth of a cent per pound?

MR. BLOUGH: Mr. Chairman, I will try to go over this again so perhaps I can communicate. My concept is that a price that matches a price is a competitive price. If you don't choose to accept that concept, then, of course, you don't accept it. In the steel industry we know it is so. . . .

There are lots of situations where the prices are different at the present time. Right now I could name a city where the price of a very important product is $5 a ton higher than our price, by a big producer.

SEN. KEFAUVER: That being the case, if the prices are different, that is not competition?

MR. BLOUGH: I would say that the buyer in that situation

who has a choice—remember now, I am talking about our published prices—the buyer in that situation has this choice. He chooses to buy from one company at $5 higher. He chooses to buy from our company at $5 lower. Now if you call that competition or a desirable form of competition, you may have it your own way. I say the buyer has more choice when the other fellow's price matches our price. . . .

Now, again, your concept of competition, that one price has to be lower than another price at all times in order to be considered competitive is simply not a practical, acceptable definition of competition in any business that I know of in the United States. It is a concept of some people who aren't familiar with business, but it is just not a practical way of running any kind of long-range, competitive manufacturing operation.

Means quotes *Time* magazine as summarizing this phase of the hearings in the following terms: "U.S. Steel Chairman Roger Blough offered another defense [of uniform prices], which would appeal to all lovers of Alice in Wonderland, and which seemed to defy the basic principle of a competitive economy. If all steel prices are the same, he contended, then the customer is free to buy from any producer he chooses. But if prices are different, then the buyer has no real freedom of choice because he must buy from the company that sells the cheapest."

Small wonder that I. F. Stone wrote that Kefauver's administered price hearings were "an eye-opener to our economic realities, and paid off richly in curbing steel and drug prices. Behind the scenes, a mere inquiry from his antitrust subcommittee was often enough to stop a corporate steal."

Kefauver was thoroughly aware, however, of the limitations of exposure in a nation whose executive branch was dominated by the golfing partners of the leading corporate executives (often they were not partners, but one and the same; when Eisenhower's Secretary of the Treasury, George M. Humphrey, resigned, he became Board Chairman George M. Humphrey of National Steel Corporation) . He was aware that the mass media (interlocked in ownership with the same executives) were far less anxious to publicize business conspiracies than they had been to publicize underworld conspiracies.

The best that Kefauver could do—and it was so much better than what anyone else was doing that it shines like a beacon light—was to expose precisely these inconsistencies.

SEN. KEFAUVER: So you have an economical operation, an efficient company, operating at low cost. Why would it not be in line with what you were working for as Secretary of the Treasury—that is, in bringing about deflation and lowering of prices—for you to pass on to the steel consumers the benefit of your operation, your greater efficiency?

MR. HUMPHREY: We do not know that we can at the present time, and we have no intention of making a move until we know what we can do.

Kefauver led the chairman of National Steel—who as Secretary of the Treasury had spoken out against raising prices—to expose the phoniness of his earlier appeals:

SEN. KEFAUVER: Suppose the low man raised his price to $25. Would you feel ashamed of yourself if you did not get your price up to $25?

MR. HUMPHREY: I would think that if the low man went to $25, there would be some very good reason for his doing so. And if the reasons that affected him in doing so affected all the rest of the industry in doing so, it would probably affect me in doing so. It would mean that something had happened that required a substantial increase in price, and if it were justified, then I would feel very badly if I could not get it. If it was unjustified, it would not last a minute.

SEN. KEFAUVER: Would you be ashamed of yourself if you did not get $25?

MR. HUMPHREY: I would be ashamed of myself if I could not get the price that was justified, that conditions justified, yes, sir, that other people could get.

Kefauver's conclusion was blunt: "As I interpret that, Mr. Humphrey, you would be ashamed of yourself if you did not get what the traffic would bear."

As for the media, Kefauver was accustomed to being misrepresented and maligned. When he reacted to unfavorable articles and cartoons, it was not with the rage of a Harry Truman or the self-pity of a Richard Nixon, but with the kind of sad grin that made it so difficult for even his enemies to dislike him. Late in 1957, after the steel-price hearings, a cartoonist on a Tennessee paper drew a sketch of Estes Kefauver standing behind Albert Gore, both of them drilling into a wall labeled "Constitutional Safeguards." He received a letter from Kefauver that said:

This is the first time that I can remember seeing myself in one of your cartoons without a coonskin cap flopping over one ear or a cigarette dangling from my mouth.

Furthermore, this is the first time I have seen any

cartoon of yours depicting someone boring away at our constitutional safeguards in which I wasn't the front borer. What's the matter? You getting softhearted or something?

With best regards.

Sincerely,
Estes Kefauver

The following year, with the active aid and cooperation of Walter Reuther, President of the United Auto Workers, his subcommittee made an exhaustive inquiry into the state of affairs in the auto industry—largest single consumer of steel, and dominated by three major corporations—one of them, General Motors, the largest in the world. Here is how *I. F. Stone's Weekly* of November 17, 1958, summed up that inquiry:

When Senator Kefauver a few years ago proceeded to expose some of the hoodlums who prey on the fringes of our society, TV and the press made him the hero of a latter-day saga. When he turned his attention to major rackets, to the uneconomic practices that affect not beer and slot machines but steel and automobiles, a blanket of silence descended upon the inquiry. The American economy pivots upon the automobile; its prospective sales are the best index of business activity; the price of cars, their financing, the level of trade-in values, are prime topics in every American home. Yet, when Kefauver as chairman of the Senate Judiciary Subcommittee on Monopoly a few days ago released a 300-page report on its investigation of the automotive industry, the first of its kind in twenty years, it briefly hit the front pages of the better newspapers and was quickly buried. Coverage was superficial; comment almost nonexistent. No TV cameras were trained on the intrepid Senator from Tennessee as he explained how the American consumer was being bilked by the longest, flashiest, and silliest cars in our history.

The auto report, largely the work of the subcommittee's chief economist, Dr. John Blair, is more than an economic analysis. It is a portrait of our society. It will be a joy to the anthropologist with a sense of humor; no primitive tribe exhibits odder folkways. The intricately planned irrationality and calculated wastefulness of our leading industry is here laid bare for the social psychiatrist. In it are the keys to our future, our hopes for orderly social evolution in America, and for peace.

At the very onset of the inquiry, Walter Reuther explained to the subcommittee why his union had been trying for two and a half years "to get the U.S. Congress to take a good look at the wage-price-profit equation in the automotive industry and especially on the part of the Big Three."

"We believe that the impact of their administered prices, the fact that they can in the exercise of their monopoly position set aside the laws of supply and demand and rig their prices," Reuther testified, "short-change American consumers, farmers, and workers. . . . We believe that investigation into the destructive impact of administered prices in America's basic industries—auto, steel, petroleum, and other critical industries—relates very directly to the source of the developing imbalance in the American economy."

By the time their inquiry was completed, the subcommittee had, to be sure, revealed the same Alice in Wonderland situation it had exposed in the steel industry. In the fall of 1956 Ford announced prices on its 1957 models averaging an increase of 2.9 per cent. Two weeks later, GM announced prices on the 1957 Chevrolet averaging an increase of 6.1 per cent. A week later Ford revised its own prices upward to meet those of Chevrolet, which led Kefauver to ask Ford Vice President Theodore O. Yntema a few pointed questions:

SEN. KEFAUVER: If you had kept your prices lower, might not Chevrolet have come to meet yours?
MR. YNTEMA: Conceivably it would have happened.
SEN. KEFAUVER: If you had kept yours lower, would you not have gotten more sales, more business?
MR. YNTEMA: Probably some more.

As I. F. Stone commented in his *Weekly,* "A candid answer would have invited antitrust prosecution. A handful of men at the top of GM determine prices and the others follow the leader—or else. GM's notion of free enterprise is strikingly like Khrushchev's; it consists of decentralizing administration under central planning and control."

In addition to these revelations about pricing policies, the Kefauver Subcommittee exposed the hoax of "higher labor costs" as the cause of steadily rising auto prices: "Labor costs have been the excuse, not the real occasion," summarized Stone's *Weekly,* "for the steady inflation of automobile prices. Hourly rated labor costs only take from $300 to $400 of a car with a factory sale value of $2,213. We are confronted with a drive to sell the public less quality at more cost."

More, the subcommittee revealed the hollowness of the auto industry's assertion that the irrational horsepower race and the ludicrous annual styling changes were simply the result of what Harlow H. Curtice, President of GM, claimed to the subcommittee: "I would say that the application of fancification to our automobiles is the result of the demand on the part of the public." He was refuted by solid evidence indicating that "demand" for souped-up engines and styling razzle-dazzle (which meant transportation that was inferior but tremendously profitable) was being artificially stimulated by wildly expensive advertising campaigns—which in themselves added an extra $100 to the cost of the average car.

The subcommittee took advantage of the resentment of American Motors, the last of the independent auto manufacturers, desperately floundering in the wake of GM, Ford, and Chrysler. George Romney, then President of American Motors, testified of the Big Three that "they introduced wraparound windshields that do not significantly improve vision and made them a hallmark of modern design. A small company could not have made the wraparound windshield a successful thing because when you get right down to the guts of it, it has no basic advantages over the straight windshield, and yet through advertising and promotion you can make an item of that type become absolutely the hallmark of a modern car, if you have got a large enough percentage of the total market to do it."

If Kefauver was not capturing the headlines now, he was laying the indispensable groundwork for Ralph Nader's subsequent muckraking attack on the automobile industry. Consider these excerpts from the subcommittee's final report:

Second only to the annual model change in importance in the field of style has been the horsepower race. . . . The lowest-priced 1958 models actually exceed in horsepower the Cadillacs, Lincolns, and Chryslers of 1950. . . .

To contain such large power plants, the cars themselves are larger in size and heavier, as are the essential automotive parts. The added cost of increased size is not, however, limited to the original purchase price. Nearly all such cars require premium fuel or they will knock considerably. In addition, overall milage seldom exceeds 12 or 13 miles per gallon.

Larger tires are required. On top of this, repair bills for even minor breakdowns tend to run high, not only for parts replacement but for the skilled labor necessary for such complex mechanisms. . . . The horsepower race is one of the major factors responsible for the present high price structure in the automobile industry and the low sales record for 1958.

Of course, it is not clear that the automobile buyers were able to determine how much of what they regarded as increased power and acceleration was in fact traceable to greater horsepower. Chrysler, for example, was disturbed by what it felt to be a common belief that other cars had a faster pickup than the Chrysler line, which Chrysler engineers said was simply untrue.

Given the problem, a market research expert reasoned that the public could not know how good an automobile's acceleration was; few people can judge the speed at which they are traveling, let alone the rate of increase in speed. Interviewers were sent out to ask car owners whether they thought their car had fast acceleration or not, and when the results were in, the tension of the spring under the accelerator pedal in each make of automobile was measured. It was found that (quoting Martin Mayer's book, *Madison Avenue, U.S.A.*), ". . . wherever the accelerator spring was tight . . . people thought the car had slow acceleration; wherever the spring was loose, people thought the chariot was blessed with get-up-and-go. Chrysler loosened the springs under the pedals."

In 1959, following the completion of the auto-industry hearings, the subcommittee decided to look into complaints by TVA that it had been getting suspiciously identical bids for heavy equipment from the nation's biggest electrical manufacturing firms. But first Kefauver found himself embroiled in a controversy over President Eisenhower's appointment of Admiral Lewis Strauss as his Secretary of Commerce.

It was not spite that motivated Estes Kefauver to oppose this appointment—his bitterest enemies were unable to make such a charge stick—or the obstructionism of a Democratic Senator seeking to hamper a Republican President. He was simply unable to dismiss from his mind the fact that, as he pointed out in a public statement,

Admiral Strauss was the chief promoter and abettor of the notorious Dixon-Yates power contract, which was a vicious attempt by private power and financial interests to undermine our fine TVA system. . . .

There is a direct conflict between the testimony of Admiral Strauss and Adolph Wenzell. There is testimony to the effect that all of the top officials in the Bureau of the Budget with whom Admiral Strauss was dealing . . . knew that Mr. Wenzell was consultant to the Bureau of the Budget. I say that it seems to me very naïve to believe, in view of all this information, that Admiral Strauss is not charged with knowledge about it himself.

The committee which held the Strauss hearings voted 9 to 8 to confirm his appointment. Kefauver voted for the minority report, which insisted: "We think the key role played by Mr. Strauss in the notorious Dixon-Yates case was a deliberate use of public office for improper aid to private business."

Kefauver was not particularly alarmed to read the fairly typical reaction of the Richmond *Times-Dispatch*: "Admiral Strauss is being insulted, and his important department demoralized, because a petty, spiteful mediocrity, Estes Kefauver, wishes to make some publicity for himself."

For one thing, his position was finally upheld in the Senate, which refused to consent to the Strauss appointment. Perhaps more important, he was used to taking stands which would expose him to insult and ridicule. At the beginning of December 1959, the sixth-grade class of a Paramus, New Jersey, school sent him one of those letters asking about his philosophy which public figures usually respond to with mimeographed platitudes. Kefauver replied:

"Keep in mind that you do not have to agree, at all times, with a majority of your associates. Many of our great patriots of the past sometimes disagreed with the majority; not because it was 'smart' to disagree but because they had honest convictions which in the long run proved to be to the best interests of the nation."

As for TVA, having beaten back the Dixon-Yates assault, it was now ready to move from the defensive to the offensive. In *The Great Price Conspiracy*, John Herling puts it like this: "One way or another, it began to express its concern about the rising prices, the identical bidding, and its general feeling that too long had it been a helpless sitting duck for the big electrical manufacturers, among others, to shoot at.

It literally had been paying too high a price for its silence."

Accordingly, late in 1959 the Kefauver Subcommittee held hearings in Knoxville to take testimony from TVA and local Tennessee utility-board employees about their experience with the bidding and pricing practices of the electrical manufacturing companies. Once transcripts had been transmitted to the Justice Department, the hearings were halted.

Kefauver was "putting the executive branch of government on notice," as Richard Austin Smith has written in *Corporations in Crisis,* "that if it didn't get on with the job, the legislative branch would." Fortunately, the Antitrust Division of the Justice Department was headed by Acting Assistant Attorney General Robert A. Bicks, not only dogged, but vigorous and competent.

Bicks and his staff proved, in months of painstaking detective work, that key officials of the largest electrical manufacturing corporations had been engaged in a conspiracy to violate the Sherman Antitrust Act and to cheat the American people out of millions, through secret meetings complete with code phrases like those of the gangland mobsters earlier exposed by Kefauver.

The unfolding of that detective work has been summarized briefly in Richard Austin Smith's book, and exhaustively in Herling's *The Great Price Conspiracy,* which reads like a mystery story. Herling says that the process of correlation

was a huge and back-breaking task. An antitrust case usually challenges the vast sweep of power that every great company trails like a cloud of glory, and you can hardly touch the corporate body anywhere without making nerves jump in far-off reaches of the body economic. Now, there came the necessity of doing the obvious before probing for the more difficult or elusive fact. From the fifty or so companies involved in the manufacture of electrical equipment, the Antitrust Division began to garner the raw data of corporate life: the organization charts, the chain of command and the chain of the commanded, the prices charged for various products, and especially the relationships with other companies through formal and informal associations of various kinds.

While there would be little doubt that the massive pressure of the TVA and the Kefauver Subcommittee was a clinching element in galvanizing the Antitrust Division to bolder efforts, the hard, slogging work, day in and day out, began to pay off. Names, prices, dates, were carefully picked up and preserved as artifacts of corporate life.

As a result, top executives of the industry pleaded guilty in order to avoid the ugly revelations of a public trial, and threw themselves on the mercy of the court. In February 1961, Estes Kefauver himself summed up as follows:

The outcome of the government's big case against price-fixers in the electrical industry ought to have a beneficial effect on all of our big industries.

In forthright fashion, Federal Judge J. Cullen Ganey of Philadelphia sent seven top executives to jail for thirty days, put twenty-three others on five years' probation, and fined individuals and corporations a total of almost $2 million.

Before, anybody who helped to administer prices in our biggest industries felt fairly safe; he was pretty sure that if caught and convicted, he would be let off with a mere fine. Now he knows he may go to jail.

Like Judge Ganey, I find it hard to believe that the top-most officials of the firms involved in this case did not know what was going on in their companies.

This feeling is based on hearings of the Senate Anti-trust and Monopoly Subcommittee which I conducted in Knoxville in 1959. The Knoxville *News-Sentinel* had called our attention to the fact that for years TVA had been receiving identical bids on purchases of electrical equipment and other materials. Our subcommittee concluded that these practices were so widespread that top industry officials must have known about them.

We turned our findings over to the Justice Department, which later obtained the Philadelphia indictments against forty-eight individuals and thirty-two corporations—practically every large firm in the electrical equipment industry. The evidence was so concrete that almost all of the defendants pleaded guilty or threw themselves on the mercy of the court.

In effect, these defendants had been stealing from the public. But a more sobering thought is pinpointed by Judge Ganey: "This is a shocking indictment of a vast section of our economy, for what is really at stake here is the survival of the kind of economy under which America had grown to greatness, the free enterprise system."

Kefauver returned his subcommittee's attention to the electrical conspiracy in 1961. Two years after that, Senator Ralph Yarborough of Texas said on the Senate floor,

It is my considered judgment that there are not three persons working in the Government of the United States today who are more valuable to the people of the United States than was Estes Kefauver.

In the investigation of the conspiracy of the manufacturers of electrical equipment, Estes Kefauver uncovered
enough evidence of conspiracy to cause the manufacturers
to plead guilty. My home city of Austin, Texas, owns its
own electrical plant. On one piece of equipment costing
millions of dollars the electrical manufacturers had all
entered identical bids. After the Kefauver exposure, the
manufacturer, this year, reduced that bid on one piece of
equipment alone by $600,000, saving that amount for the
tax-paying and electricity-using citizens of Austin, Texas,
my home city, on only one piece of equipment.

Consider how much he meant to the whole country.

In 1959 and 1960, the Kefauver Subcommittee turned the
spotlight on the baking industry. Baking was small business
compared to the giants of the steel, automotive, and electrical world—but business which daily affected the stomach—
and the pocketbook—of every American family. Once again
the investigation centered on the effect of monopolistic
power, this time on the small businessman and the whole-
sale bread industry. And once again it disclosed "a remarkable absence of competitive pricing in most major cities."

Kefauver observed in his *In a Few Hands,*

Prices changed infrequently, and when they did, the
change was almost invariably in one direction—upward.
Price reductions were noticeably absent except in those
small and medium-sized cities where there were still some
"troublesome" independents who resisted being driven
out of their home markets. . . .

The mechanism by which prices change may vary from
time to time and place to place. The most direct method,
of course, is outright collusion. There is evidence of col-

lusion in several Department of Justice cases against bread companies in various local markets. . . .

In other cases the price leader may simply notify his competitors of his intentions to raise prices. Many instances of this practice are contained in the files of the subcommittee. . . .

In still other cases, neither collusion nor notification appears necessary. The price leader simply increases his prices. His competitors learn of this almost immediately from their route drivers and then raise their own prices to the leader's level. . . . It seems clear that the major bakers have adopted the rationale employed by other industries that practice administered pricing. When prices are raised, it is "to meet competition." . . . Like the steel producers, the large bakers regard themselves as "competitive" only when their prices are just as high as those of their brethren in the industry.

The subcommittee had reached these conclusions through careful examination of such practices as plant discrimination and route discrimination. Perhaps the most fascinating is that of "stales clobbering," both for its clear picture of ordinary American business practices and for its revelation of how those practices affected ordinary people. Here is Kefauver's own summary:

In the baking industry stale bread which is unsold is customarily returned to the baker, and the grocer is reimbursed for his stale returns. Obviously, it is to the baker's interest to sell as much as possible but to hold stale returns to a minimum. On the other hand, it is generally accepted in the trade that consumers are influenced by the "pile psychology"; that is, they tend to select a loaf from the largest pile on the grocery shelf. Thus a conflict is created. Though the baker wishes to keep stale returns to a minimum, he feels he must maintain a respectable pile on the grocer's bread rack to entice the customers. The large pile also has another advantage; it crowds the wares of the smaller independents off the shelves.

After describing how the market is "slugged" with more merchandise than can possibly be sold, both to attract customers and to force rival merchandise off the limited shelf space, Kefauver goes on:

This game tends to be one-sided. The larger companies are financially able to squeeze the independents by flooding the grocery stores with their brands and absorbing the losses on stales. The small baker is in a dilemma. He can match the practices of his bigger competitors or lose volume. In either event, he is bound to suffer. If he tries to match piles with the bigger companies, his stale returns will increase dramatically and his profits will be reduced to a minimum. If he remains aloof from this form of competitive activity, his sales volume falls.

Here is another form of competitive activity in which there is no real gain to the public. The studied creation of mountains of stale bread serves no useful end to society; nor is there any social benefit to be derived by catering to the fiction that the height of the pile is an indication to the consumer of the freshness of the bread.

Had drug-industry executives paid even minimal attention to these bread-industry hearings, which were being concluded even while preparations were under way in the Kefauver Subcommittee for the big drug inquiry, they would not have made the mistake of so many monopolists before them.

Fortunately for us all, Kefauver selected *New Yorker* staff writer Richard Harris to cover the drug hearings, and in the process confided in him with unusual frankness. In his history of the hearings, *The Real Voice,* which appeared in 1964, Harris quotes a drug-industry lobbyist as recalling: "They thought they'd come in there with all that high-priced legal and public relations talent and mop up the floor with him. They simply refused to believe that he was tough and small as hell."

During the bread hearings the subcommittee staff had consisted of some thirty-eight people, both professional and clerical. While the bread inquiry was drawing to a conclusion eight of them—notably, economist Dr. John Blair; his assistant, Dr. Irene Till; Mrs. Lucile Burd Wendt, a bacteriologist-chemist-lawyer; and Dr. E. Wayles Browne, a statistical economist—had been concentrating on preparing preliminary material concerning the drug industry.

In July 1959, the bread hearings wound up, and shortly thereafter Kefauver announced that open hearings on the drug industry would begin in December. He was ready to undertake what would be—although he had no way of knowing it—the greatest challenge of his life, and the one with the most profound consequences for the American people.

ten ☆ The Final Challenge

☆☆☆ In the fall of 1959, Estes Kefauver was looking forward confidently to an investigation of drug-pricing practices that would climax his committee's earlier inquiries. He had a staff that was the envy of the Congress. His technicians had already analyzed subpoenaed documents from the drug companies (and were "stunned" by how little the stuff cost that the public was being charged such astronomical prices for) ; and he had reason to believe—as he had not in the steel and auto inquiries—that for the first time since the crime hearings he would be able to reach out to all of America with this story.

The reason was simple. As Paul Rand Dixon, his staff director and chief counsel, had indicated, the press was more free when it did not have to worry about advertisers. Since ethical drug companies did not advertise their products in newspapers, the papers felt freer to report fully on matters connected with prescription products.

The pressure was coming not from the advertisers, but from the people. Once again Kefauver had touched the right nerve: He was not the only one who felt outraged at having to overpay for a handful of pills, his staff were not alone in their indignation at learning that all antibiotics were selling at the same exact price. Ordinary people all over the country had been waiting for someone to take up the fight against exorbitant drug prices. Their letters started coming in at the rate of a dozen a day, and spiraled up to several hundred a day.

"The people thought of Estes Kefauver as a protector," Senator Philip Hart of Michigan, a freshman committee member during the drug investigation, has said. "Common people everywhere—and perhaps not without some justification—have the feeling that there are great and powerful forces allied against their best interests. But having a man like Estes Kefauver around did a lot to relieve their feeling of helplessness."

Counterpressure to the public pleas for relief from high prices for essential drugs came from doctors, druggists, chambers of commerce, and, most importantly, from retail-drug associations. Before the battle was over the pharmaceutical manufacturers were to sink $5 million into the anti-Kefauver Committee battle (for which they would be reimbursed by a new tax bill making lobbyists' expenses deductible) . September 21, 1959, *Drug Trade News*: "Lately there have been reports that Senator Kefauver, who faces an uphill battle for re-election next year, was being urged to drop the inquiry entirely."

"Estes kept asking me," Dixon told Richard Harris, " 'Is it right? Is it in the public interest? Does it need to be done?' After all that the staff had come up with, I couldn't answer anything but 'Yes' each time. Estes finally said, 'Well, then, we had better go ahead.' "

On December 7, 1959, the subcommittee hearings got under way. On the very first day it became clear that the captains of the drug industry were every bit as ruthless—and as unprepared for Kefauver's searching queries—as the steel and auto tycoons had been.

The first witness was Francis C. Brown, President of the

Schering Corporation. After his opening statement, he was asked by Paul Rand Dixon, in reference to prednisolone (synthesized cortisone, used by arthritis victims), "Do you consider it reasonable on your part to charge 17.9 cents for a tablet when your cost certainly must be less than 1.6 cents?"

In his response, just as the auto makers had fallen back on "public demand" for "fancified" cars, Mr. Brown fell back on what was to be the standard drug-company refrain: "research." But Kefauver was ready for this:

> Let's get it very clear. You buy this material from Upjohn. . . . All you do is put it in a capsule, add your brand name to it, and sell it. Presumably, this $2.37 price per gram . . . includes research costs, with some profit remaining for Upjohn. So presumably at $2.37 a gram you can produce it and include research and profit and depreciation and whatnot in it also. Upjohn could not under the law sell it to you at a loss. They must sell it to you at a profit. We have a reliable concern here that will tablet it for $2 per thousand tablets . . . so that your maximum cost per bottle of one hundred, which must include some research and some profit, is $1.57. Yet you sell it for $17.90. How do you justify that?

It was quickly becoming clear to Mr. Brown, and to his brothers in the industry, that they were in for trouble. John Blair produced figures to indicate that the markup on prednisolone alone was 1,118 per cent. He followed them up with a chart indicating that the four largest companies selling prednisolone all charged the same prices. Brown's response was weirdly similar to that of the electrical-industry conspirators—that the competitive situation required those prices.

SEN. KEFAUVER: I have never understood this kind of a competitive system. How is it, if you want to be really competitive, you don't lower your price to get more of the business?

MR. BROWN: Senator, we can't put two sick people in every bed where there is only one person sick.

At this a representative of the drug industry got up and left the room. Later he told Richard Harris that he never expected to hear anyone in the business testify that drug prices were high because the number of sick people was limited.

In the ten months of testimony from some hundred and fifty witnesses that followed this first sensational day, Kefauver slowly built his case, with a knowledge of complicated terminology and technical data that impressed and even astonished observers. He was going to frame a bill that would protect consumers—the sick, the old, patients in hospitals, young parents—from a whole series of abuses. It became clear that administered prices, so high that they forced some purchasers to choose between food and desperately needed drugs, were far from the only abuse. We can do no more than sketch some of the others in the paragraphs that follow.

Research was exposed for what it all too often was: In the words of Dr. Frederick H. Meyers, of the University of California Medical School, it was used "mostly to modify the original drug just enough to get a patentable derivative." Not only was much of it devoted to marketing drugs that were useless or worse, the research expenditures of the entire drug industry were hardly any more than the amount spent annually on research grants by the National Institutes of Health, a government agency.

Patents turned out to be a key factor in keeping drug prices artificially high. Private deals were made between the major drug companies to license each other manufacturing and sales rights; when (as a consequence of the Kefauver hearings) the Federal Trade Commission found five big firms guilty of conspiring to fix tetracycline prices, it charged that "unclean hands and bad faith played a major role" in the private arrangements.

Advertising to the medical profession was shown to be wildly expensive. According to Richard Harris, the subcommittee staff estimated that in 1958 the industry must have spent at least $750 million on advertising. It was more like an avalanche than a reasonable educational service to doctors. A Salt Lake City obstetrician, after weighing his drug mail for two months with a postal scale, testified: "It would take 2 railroad cars, 110 large mail trucks, and 800 postmen to deliver the daily load of drug circulars and samples to doctors if mailed to a single city." The subcommittee's subpoenaed records showed that an average of 24 per cent of the companies' gross income had gone for advertising and promotion.

Insistence on trade names was used both to keep prices high and to confuse the medical profession as well as the public. The prescribing of drugs by trademarked name rather than by chemical or generic name served to "snow" the consumer, who had no way of knowing that the same product was available for a fraction of the price under its original rather than its brand name.

Misuse of antibiotics and inadequate warning of their possible dangers were both widespread and dangerous. In 1951, Parke, Davis had sold $52 million of Chloromycetin, which doctors were prescribing for just about everything.

When it became public knowledge that the drug was causing dangerous blood abnormalities, including aplastic anemia, the Food and Drug Administration ordered the company to print the following warning:

> Certain blood dyscrasias (aplastic anemia, thrombocytopenic purpura, granulocytopenia, and pancytopenia) have been associated with the administration of Chloromycetin. It is essential that adequate blood studies be made when prolonged or intermittent administration of this drug is required. Chloromycetin should not be used indiscriminately or for minor infections.

Within three years thereafter, Chloromycetin sales had dropped by $17 million. But in 1960, when Harry J. Loynd, President of Parke, Davis, came before the Kefauver Subcommittee, sales were all the way up to $86 million. In the intervening years, Kefauver observed, the company had changed the wording of the warning in its direct-mail promotion so that it read like this:

> Chloromycetin is a potent therapeutic agent and, because certain blood dyscrasias have been associated with its administration, it should not be used indiscriminately or for minor infections. Furthermore, as with certain other drugs, adequate blood studies should be made when the patient requires prolonged or intermittent therapy.

SEN. KEFAUVER: I am afraid that what you have done here is first to dilute the first part of this warning, which starts off "Certain blood dyscrasias have been associated," by putting in front of that "Chloromycetin is a potent therapeutic agent." Then you have diluted the blood-study part by saying, "As with certain other drugs." You give the impression that certain other drugs have the same requirement. Then you have diluted "essential" by putting in "should be."

Government regulatory agencies were revealed as little more than working partners of the firms they were supposed to be regulating in the public interest. The Kefauver Subcommittte found the FDA less than helpful; as for its commissioner, George P. Larrick, he was prone to boast of his good relations with friends in the industry. Dr. Barbara Moulton testified as to why she had resigned after five years as a drug examiner with the FDA: "The Food and Drug Administration has failed utterly in its solemn task of enforcing those sections of the law dealing with the safety and misbranding of drugs, particularly prescription drugs."

Before he could draw up a bill, however, or even complete the hearings, Kefauver had to get home to Tennessee for the summer 1960 primaries. With the coming of a new decade, he had given up his dream of aiming for the Presidency. There remained the job of winning re-election—really a pleasure, for he drew a kind of strength from ambling down the Tennessee streets, ready to shake the hands of all comers.

For all his concentration on the knotty economic problems, Kefauver had hardly been neglecting the folks down home. The great handshaker had always made it a practice to address at least one high school commencement every year, to salute disc jockey festivals in Nashville (and the country music which has meant so much to the state capital) , and to send Senatorial congratulations to the graduating sons and daughters of his constituents. In his office sat a little old lady from Tennessee named Miss White, whose task it was to go through all of the hometown papers and write "the dead letters"—a note of condolence to every bereaved family in the state. Between thirty and forty of these letters lay on the Senator's desk at the end of every day, awaiting his signature. Charles Caldwell remembers how someone once said, rather shocked, "Estes, what a terrible thing to do." And how Kefauver replied, "Not at all. When people are troubled it's all I can do as their Senator." It was a mixture, Caldwell thought, of good politics and simple kindness.

When he got to Tennessee, a public opinion poll had already indicated that he was running far behind his primary opponent, who was carrying on a miserable racist campaign against him. He was going to need all of his magnetic kindness and political savvy to pull through, but until the last week before the August primary it did not look as though those qualities would be enough. Not when doctors and druggists were mailing out thousands of leaflets with their bills, describing the Senator as a radical determined to ruin Americans' health. Only after the news weeklies wrote him off as a losing candidate did "scared" money begin to pour into his campaign headquarters—too late to use effectively.

Martha Ragland traveled with him on as much of his killing schedule as she could take. "I felt battle fatigue, exhaustion, in his campaigning. He didn't have the stamina he'd had before, but he continued to drive himself, giving dull talks that people traveled hundreds of miles to hear. The columnist Mary McGrory was close to the mark when she wrote that people didn't come to listen to him so much as to drink him in."

Was he getting through to his people with those dull talks?

It seemed doubtful, not when he was being assaulted yet again as a "nigger-lover and a Red." Richard Harris describes the climax:

Then, one day toward the close of the campaign, he was giving his more or less standard speech in a small town when the local druggist came out of his store, at the rear of the crowd, and began heckling him. At first, Kefauver ignored the man, but when he persisted, the Senator began citing facts and figures about the high costs of drugs. Suddenly, in a unique display of oratorical fervor, he flung out a long arm with forefinger pointed at the druggist, and cried, "There's one of your enemies!" The audience roared its approval, and there were shouts of "Give it to him, Estes!" From then on, Kefauver made all of his speeches within pointing distance of the local drugstore, and used the same line and gesture, with much the same results. In the end, the pollsters, most of the Tennessee press, the drug industry, and Kefauver himself were astonished when he rolled up a 2-to-1 victory.

Now he was free to wind up the hearings without the specter of political annihilation. What was more, the narrow Presidential victory that fall of his former rival, Jack Kennedy, over his old opponent, Dick Nixon, seemed to ensure White House support of the drug bill that he and his staff proceeded to draw up. He could hardly have foreseen that, in the biggest irony of all, the New Frontiersmen who came so gaily and confidently to Washington would sabotage him, in collaboration with the right-wing Republicans who had dominated the scene during the previous decade and mocked his efforts to protect plain people from corporate rapacity.

Throughout the earlier hearings Senator Everett Dirksen had, in the words of *The New Republic* magazine, "taken on himself the burden of defending America's medical and pharmaceutical interests for the Republican party." His fellow Republican on the subcommittee, Senator Roman Hruska of Nebraska, "defended everything the industry had ever done and attacked the least significant criticisms of it at endless length," a drug-industry representative told Richard Harris, "instead of concentrating on the drug industry's considerable achievements and letting the ugly facts pass by as quickly and unobtrusively as possible."

"In all my years in Congress," Kefauver commented, "I've never encountered such harassment, obstructionism, and vilification."

The elections out of the way, Kefauver utilized the hearings (despite the Dirksen-Hruska efforts) to nail down proof of the need for a drug bill that would lower prices, increase competition, and protect the health of the layman. As he wrote in his *In a Few Hands,* "the ultimate consumer—the patient—is captive. The doctor, in writing the prescription, places the order for the merchandise; the consumer foots the bill. Thus the man who orders does not pay, and the man who pays does not order."

The man who ordered, the doctor, as Kefauver demonstrated irrefutably, was often misled not only by the drug companies, but by endorsements from his own professional organization. He had Dr. Irene Till take the stand to read a statement from the *Journal* of the American Medical Association: "Every statement that appears in AMA publication ads must be backed by substantiated facts . . . or we won't run it! This is why you can rely on what you read about products that are advertised in the pages of AMA scientific journals."

Dr. Till then read two advertisements from the *Journal,* one for Equanil, one for Miltown—the same drug, marketed under different names.

The Equanil ad:

"Careful supervision of dose and amount prescribed is advised, especially for patients with a known propensity for taking excessive quantities of drugs. Excessive and prolonged use in susceptible persons (alcoholics, former addicts, and other severe psychoneurotics) has been reported to result in dependence on the drug."

The Miltown ad:

"Simple dosage schedule produces rapid, reliable tranquilization without unpredictable excitation

"No cumulative effects, thus no need for difficult dosage readjustments

"Does not produce depression, Parkinson-like symptoms, jaundice, or agranulocytosis

"Does not impair mental efficiency or normal behavior."

In April of 1961 Kefauver submitted his drug bill to the Senate, even though hearings were to continue on into February 1962, lasting over two years and filling nearly 13,000 pages with testimony. "The Senator is a persistent if quixotic man," wrote Milton Viorst at the time in the magazine *The Nation.* "Perhaps in the end his notion of what is relevant may be nearer the mark than that of the mass media that have so long dismissed him as a crank."

In April and May of 1961 Kefauver turned his subcommittee's attention once more to the great price conspiracy of the electrical industry.

Inasmuch as the second-rank managers of such concerns as GE and Westinghouse had pleaded guilty and thrown themselves on the mercy of the court, there had been simple sentences and fines, but no jury trials which might have provided the public with that educational exposure to business methods which was Kefauver's great specialty. Kefauver now proceeded to demonstrate—despite the continuous intervention of Senators Dirksen and Hruska on behalf of the electrical executives—that responsibility did not stop with the second-rank managers, but went all the way to the top. John Herling's account of the interrogation of William S. Ginn, Vice President of General Electric until March 16, 1961, gives us a good idea of how Kefauver utilized understatement and quiet questioning to educate everyone who would listen on the facts of American business life:

When he left Schenectady to go to jail, [Ginn] had no idea that this might prove the end of his General Electric career. He issued this "farewell address" through the *GE Schenectady News* of February 10, 1961:

"My fellow employees and friends: All of you know that next Monday in Philadelphia, I shall start serving a thirty-day jail term, along with six other businessmen in the electrical industry, for conduct that has been interpreted as being in conflict with the complex antitrust laws.

"The purpose of this message is not to re-argue the case or protest the sentence. The record has been written and the book is closed. Rather I write to remind you that General Electric, Schenectady, and its people have undergone many ordeals together and we have not only survived them, but we have come out stronger, more vigorous, more alive than ever. We shall again. . . ."

Later on Ginn threw some light on his feelings toward GE. "When I got out being a guest of the government for thirty days, I had found out that we were not going to be paid while we were there, and I got, frankly, madder than hell, and I called—I couldn't get hold of Mr. Linder [the group vice president], so I called Mr. Cordiner, and he told me:

" 'Bill, the best thing for you to do, now you have been under stress, go down to Florida for a week with your family and then you come up here and I want to talk to you.'

"When I came up and talked to him on the 16th of March, he said that he felt that in the best interests of myself and the company, that I should resign, and I told him in a split second, 'I agree.' "

As Ginn finished telling his story the atmosphere in the Senate room grew tense. This was the story of an organization man being cut down—by the organization.

Senator Kefauver said: "Well, nobody can condone what you or any of the people in your line of command did, but I certainly have the feeling that with this thing going on widely in business as you have related—none of you should have met with competitors—but you were directed from higher up. It looks like pretty rough treatment you fellows got."

"Well, Senator"—Ginn tried to speak.

"I know Westinghouse has acknowledged being a corporate failure as the others have. I do not understand the holier-than-thou attitude in GE when your directions came from very high at the top. But I do not ask you to comment unless you want to," Kefauver said.

Ginn grinned: "I think it would be just as well if I don't."

"If you did comment," Kefauver said, "what would you say?"

The caucus room burst into laughter.

"Speaking for me personally, Senator," Ginn said, "this is the way the ball has bounced. I have learned a good lesson. I hope that I will have the opportunity to continue in American industry and do a job. I think that some of the other boys may have possibly had a rougher deal, and I want to leave the company with no bitterness and to go out and see if I can't start a new venture along the right lines."

The room was dead quiet when Ginn ended. "Well, I admire your desire and your attitude, but you fellows were taking a lot of blame you were directed to do, and a lot of punishment, you and your family, did you not?" said Senator Kefauver.

"By the same token," Mr. Ginn rallied, "a man has got to realize that he should not compromise his principles even though he is told to do so, and I think we have got to share some of the blame ourselves."

"Well, I think you have got to, but not all of it," Senator Kefauver replied.

Kefauver had proceeded in similar fashion with the President of the Westinghouse Corporation, Mark W. Cresap, Jr. Once again he utilized the testimony to teach the American people how the great corporations really functioned. As Herling recounts it:

The more than $17-million price both companies [GE and Westinghouse] offered as identical secret bids occurred in 1958. Then, Senator Kefauver produced an-

other price list published by General Electric. The date
for this price tag was March 1961; the price was $12,000,-
070 for the same electrical machinery. Senator Kefauver
dryly remarked: "The prices have gone down very
rapidly." (The price was lower, but the identity lingered
on.)

"It has exactly the same description as the machine that
both of you offered to make for $17,402,300. Neither of
you has made one yet, but here their price is now at a
little more than $12 million. Is that your price, Mr.
Cresap?"

"Yes, Senator, and it is a very low price," said Cresap.

"How do you know?" snapped Kefauver.

"Well," said Cresap, somewhat huffily, "I know what
the costs are on these machines, sir, and I know this is a
very special price."

"But you have no breakdown. We asked Mr. William
H. Eckert, your lawyer, and he said there was no breakdown."

"Of course there are breakdowns on costs. You can't
be in the manufacturing business without having breakdowns on costs."

"Well," said Senator Kefauver, "will you supply this
in confidence to the committee? We have been trying for
three weeks to get the breakdown, and Mr. Eckert says
there is no breakdown. Is that correct, Mr. Eckert?"

This placed the Westinghouse lawyer directly on the
spot, but he replied evenly, looking ahead, without glanc-
ing at his client, the Westinghouse president: "It is my
understanding that Westinghouse had no breakdown on
the figure of $17,402,300 with which it started its list for
that Colbert (TVA) job."

"That is what you told us and that is what I said," said

the Tennessee Senator. Turning his attention to Cresap, he asked: "Then, Mr. Cresap, do you have a breakdown that you never told your lawyers about?"

"No, sir," said Cresap.

Now Senator Kefauver rubbed it in a little harder. "Are we going to be in the situation from now on as we have in the past, in spite of your fine statement here about costs independently arrived at, of at least the two big companies having the same price day in and day out?"

"No, sir," said Cresap. He explained that on particular job specifications, the prices arrived at would be entirely different. "The book price," he said, "is a basis for determining the actual price, and the prices change constantly."

Kefauver slogged on. He pointed out that "identity" persisted: Westinghouse and General Electric had both deducted from the sealed bids exactly the same amount— $177,900—for the item of "supervision" which TVA decided it was going to handle itself.

"So on sealed bids, you both subtracted, for lack of supervision, exactly the same figure, $177,900, to the penny. How do you account for that?"

"I am not familiar with the calculation having to do with those bids," Cresap said. He explained that he was president of a $2-billion company and the product line under discussion came to less than 5 per cent of the total volume. Since he was not an engineer, he was not in the position of going into the intricacies of pricing on turbine generators, and he therefore had to rely on his people who understood these things.

"I know," said Senator Kefauver, "but you are president of the company, and you say that nothing ever came to your attention that would put you on notice of any collusive action. How in the world would you explain how on a sealed bid, where TVA said they didn't want supervision in the erection of the turbo-steam generator, both you and General Electric would subtract $177,900? Is there any way that you could do it without talking it over?"

"I haven't the slightest idea," Cresap answered. . . .

"It is a great deal more pleasant to ask you questions about light and goodness and not ask any questions that are critical in any way," said Senator Kefauver, "but it is the job of this committee to investigate antitrust and monopoly and try to be an influence to help bring about competition in American industry. . . ."

Kefauver wound up his probing of Cresap in his best avuncular manner:

"It is true, as you have stated, that Westinghouse has done many fine things and we want your company to be a wholesome, independent competitor, which I am afraid it hasn't been at all times in the past, free from violation of the law, and we will be watching to see what happens."

"All right, sir," said Cresap, "I welcome the spotlight on Westinghouse."

"You think it is a good thing?" asked Kefauver beaming.

"Yes, sir," said Cresap, sweating, and forcing a little smile.

If the president of Westinghouse thought that the spotlight was a good thing, it was not clear that the President of the United States did also. "The President," says Bernard Nossiter, chief economics writer for the Washington *Post,* in his book *The Mythmakers,* "had displayed a cool indifference to the attempt of Senator Estes Kefauver of Tennessee to make a close and possibly embarrassing study of steel costs and profits."

To understand the reason for this "cool indifference"—which would plague the final months of Kefauver's life and threaten to destroy his carefully written drug bill—we must recall President Kennedy's difficulties with the steel industry. Like its predecessors, and indeed like its successors down through the Nixon administration in the 1970's, the Kennedy administration had built its economic policy around the notion of controlling inflation by urging wage "restraint" upon the steelworkers' union and price "restraint" upon the steel manufacturers. (The end result of this policy—runaway inflation accompanied by a depressed economy and increasing unemployment—finally forced President Nixon to abandon it in favor of a wage and price freeze.)

With rumors increasing that the industry was going to announce a price increase, in the fall of 1962 President Kennedy sent a public letter to the heads of the twelve leading steel companies, promising them, in effect, that if they would not raise their prices he would use his influence on the steel union to keep its demands low. And when they refrained from announcing a price increase, the President and his Secretary of Labor, Arthur Goldberg (who had been general counsel to the steelworkers' union), met secretly with the president of the union and the President of U.S. Steel, Roger Blough. The union settled for its smallest gain since World War II.

Within ten days after the signing of this new contract, however, Roger Blough announced that Big Steel would be raising its prices about $6 a ton—and the President of the United States turned on him in fury, demanding that the increase be rescinded.

"There is a touch of irony in this affair," comments Nossiter. "According to the conventional business mind, Kennedy proved once and for all his hostility to business by cracking down on Blough. In fact, it appears that Kennedy cracked down on Blough to save a policy of wage restraint that lies near to the hearts of right-thinking businessmen." Nevertheless, the President discovered to his dismay that he had suddenly become an object of hatred to American capitalists. "At Union League Clubs, in the Duquesne Club in Pittsburgh, and in other executive fortresses, Kennedy was denounced with a fervor once reserved for Franklin Roosevelt. There was a bizarre and ugly viciousness in all this. But it had its effect. By the end of 1962, the White House was throwing out hints that selective price increases on some steel products would not be objected to."

It was also looking askance at Estes Kefauver's exposure of the drug industry. ("Net profits for Smith, Kline & French have continued to remain extraordinarily high," he reported in his *In a Few Hands,* "usually 35 per cent or more on investment after taxes. Since [their] potent tranquilizers are primarily used in mental hospitals supported by state and local governments, these monopoly profits have been made directly at the expense of the taxpayer.") Nor was the White House enthused by Kefauver's bill S. 1552, which would cut drug prices through a compulsory-licensing provision and provide clearer information by requiring that advertising describe bad as well as good effects of every drug. Kefauver was prepared for a battle from the drug industry and its Republican apologists—because of the Dirksen-Hruska opposition his bill was barely voted out by his own subcommittee. But he was hardly ready to take on his own party, and the young President in the White House.

Yet that was apparently what he faced, for in mid-March of 1962, when President Kennedy released his Consumer Message, it did not even refer to Kefauver's bill, much less to the urgent need for its passage. Taken up with playing cold war games, Kennedy and his New Frontiersmen had far more appetite for confronting Communists abroad than capitalists at home, particularly when they wished to placate the angry business community prior to the 1964 elections.

There followed a series of depressing maneuvers too complex to detail here. They are carefully described in Richard Harris's *The Real Voice*. Reviewing that book in *The Nation,* science writer Elinor Langer commented, "We always knew that Kefauver was disliked in Washington in general and that he was fought with particular intensity on the drug bill. But it was not known that the opposition was so unscrupulous or that the drug lobby was so closely linked with a quiet anti-Kefauver coalition that included not only Senate colleagues like Eastland and Dirksen, but high representatives of the White House and the Department of Health, Education and Welfare. The linen was dirtier than almost anyone imagined. . . ."

The Kennedy administration moved one day to support right-wing efforts to bury any drug legislation, the next (in response to outraged cries like those from columnist Drew Pearson) to support a weak version of the Kefauver bill. Washington *Post* writer Karl E. Meyer characterized this line as "anticipatory surrender"—that is, making a deal with your opponents after having asked for so little that you wind up getting next to nothing in return.

The climax of this maneuvering was a meeting of Mississippi's Senator James Eastland, reactionary inner club member and chairman of the Judiciary Committee (parent body of the Kefauver Subcommittee) , with some technicians from the Department of Health, Education and Welfare and a man from the Food and Drug Administration. Not only was Estes Kefauver not invited—it had been supposedly set up to work out a compromise of the legislation on which he had labored for so long—he was not even told that the secret meeting had been called.

When he learned of it, Kefauver phoned Wilbur Cohen, Assistant Secretary of Health, Education and Welfare. "It looks to me as though you were working both sides of the street," he told Cohen. "This is the first time in my twenty-three years in Congress that an administration has emasculated a bill without letting its sponsor and chairman know."

To Richard Harris, Kefauver said,

I've never been so disturbed by double-dealing in all my life. I trusted those people. They've obviously decided that it would be better to get *some* kind of a bill—the weakest possible—passed now. That way, it will be another twenty-five years before anything more is done. And if they get this new bill through, they can say to the public, "The industry was investigated thoroughly and Congress did such and such. Now you can have complete faith in drugs again." Also, I think it was the feeling on the part of the administration, especially the FDA, that they didn't want many reforms to start with. This new bill shows that they were content with the most moderate improvements. Now they can claim that they got legislation through to protect the people. At the same time, they can say to the industry, "See, we didn't do you much harm."

But Kefauver and his staff were not about to quit. That very afternoon, he jumped aboard the Senate subway from his office to the Capitol, heading for the Senate floor to denounce those who had been involved in sabotaging his bill. Learning of his intentions, the White House (in the person of Meyer Feldman, the President's deputy special counsel) phoned to warn Kefauver that his speech might be politically embarrassing for himself and the President. Kefauver replied: "I haven't been so shoddily treated in twenty-three years in Congress."

He did not remind Feldman, as he might have, that in 1960, despite his own difficult re-election campaign, he had campaigned for Kennedy in thirty states, more than any other Senator. Nor, despite the urging of his staff, did he attack the administration from the floor of the Senate, beyond asserting: "In view of the fact that representatives of the Department of Health, Education and Welfare participated in secret meetings to damage this bill seriously, I think the people are now entitled to know just how they happened to be there and what the administration's present position is."

He concentrated on exposing the secret nature of the meeting, placing his Populist faith as always in an informed and aroused public.

Much to my amazement, at a meeting of the Judiciary Committee this morning, I discovered that there had been a secret meeting between representatives of the Department of Health, Education and Welfare . . . and staff members of the Judiciary Committee representing the Senator from Mississippi and staff members of the Antitrust Subcommittee representing the Senator from Illinois and the Senator from Nebraska, of which I knew nothing. . . . Not only had there been an agreement to eliminate the remaining patent provision endorsed by

Commissioner Ladd, but there had also been an agreement to water down virtually every remaining feature of the bill. . . . The bill which now remains is a mere shadow of the one approved by the Antitrust and Monopoly Subcommittee only a few months ago. . . . I want the people to know what has been happening and what the situation is. The bill as it stands is admittedly agreeable to the Senator from Illinois and the Senator from Nebraska. They have generally, and I think admittedly, taken the position on these issues set forth by the pharmaceutical industry.

People were surprised by Kefauver's bitterness—it seemed uncharacteristic, coming from such a quiet gentleman—and inclined to bet that his drug bill was dead. Indeed, it might very well have been, if not for a terrible tragedy which Kefauver's staff was quick to capitalize upon, using its headlines to revitalize the dying drug bill.

On Sunday, July 15, 1962, the Washington *Post* carried a front-page story headlined: HEROINE OF FDA KEEPS BAD DRUG OFF MARKET. The story, written by Morton Mintz and based on an interview with Dr. Frances O. Kelsey, a medical officer on the staff of the Food and Drug Administration, disclosed that Dr. Kelsey had for months been resisting approval of a sleeping pill known as thalidomide, in common use in Europe for years. On over fifty occasions the company wishing to market the drug had been stalled by Dr. Kelsey, whose suspicions about its possible side effects had been aroused.

Just as she was nearing the end of her resistance, sensational news arrived from West Germany: The cause of a hideous epidemic of phocomelia among newborn babies had been traced to use of the sleeping pill by pregnant women. Over 7,000 babies had been born as a phocomelus. (*Webster's Dictionary*: "A monster having the arms and legs extremely short or absent, so that the hands and feet appear attached directly to the trunk.")

"If it hadn't been for Dr. Kelsey," John Blair had tipped off Washington *Post* reporters Bernard Nossiter and Morton Mintz, basing himself on the dossier on thalidomide that his staff associate Lucile Wendt had been carefully compiling, "thalidomide would have been selling here for the past year, and we'd now have a medical disaster of major proportions on our hands."

The next day, July 16, Senator Kefauver released Mrs. Wendt's thalidomide dossier to the press, which was already printing heartbreaking photographs of malformed infants. While the public was still in a state of shock and outrage, he proposed on the floor of the Senate that Dr. Kelsey be awarded the Gold Medal for Distinguished Federal Civilian Service.

A week later an American woman who had been taking thalidomide during her pregnancy went for an abortion to Sweden, where it was subsequently announced, just as she had feared, that her unborn child was deformed. On July 26 the New York *Times* editorialized: "Will the administration give Senator Kefauver some support on this issue and not confine itself to generalities about its concern for consumers?"

Now surely there would be no stopping a drug bill that would protect Americans from these horrors. President Kennedy did indeed accept Kefauver's suggestion; on August 7 he awarded the Gold Medal to Dr. Kelsey—but Kefauver ("one of the dread reformers who are decidedly out in today's Washington," in the words of columnist Doris Fleeson) was not invited to the ceremony until the last minute, and then was pushed aside by the press as it sought photos of Dr. Kelsey with the President. As for the latter's administration, its behavior in the final weeks of wheeling and dealing over a compromise drug bill can only be described as ignoble. In the Senate, the key patent-licensing provision was tabled, thus killing it—on instructions from the White House, Senator Mansfield told Senator Kefauver. In the House, Deputy Attorney General Nicholas Katzenbach reneged on a promise to the Kefauver staff to fight for a strong version of the bill.

On October 3, the bill did emerge, strengthened, from a tough battle in the final Senate-House conference, and Estes Kefauver took to the floor to sum up.

> This bill constitutes something of a tribute to the Founding Fathers for their wisdom in creating the legislative branch as a separate branch of government. . . . The bill involved new thinking, new ideas. They came from a legislative committee. At the outset of the investigation, we were actually discouraged by top officials of the Food and Drug Administration. Not only had they no remedies for most of the problems with which we were beginning to be concerned; they did not even recognize them as problems. . . . The moral of the drug bill is that even on an exceedingly complex issue the legislative branch can perform in the manner originally intended. With only a small staff of competent professional personnel, the Congress can prove itself to be just as able as the vast bureaucracy of the executive branch, if not more so, to assume leadership in the legislative process.

"What the Senator was too modest to say," Morton Mintz has written in his study of the drug industry, *The Therapeutic Nightmare,* "was that the Congress performed as it did on the drug bill because he, aided by a few other dedicated Senators and Congressmen, and by a superb staff, acted with extraordinary brilliance, courage, and tenacity. In the end, he was rescued from defeat by the thalidomide catastrophe. What the Senator was too kind to say was that some of his highly influential colleagues had actively engaged in sabotage of his efforts."

The New York *Times* saluted him as a "hero" because he had "doggedly continued to push for this needed legislation despite widespread public apathy, lack of administration interest, and bitter opposition from some industry and Congressional sources."

Kefauver was not exactly a hero to the administration. His drug bill was due to be signed by President Kennedy on October 10, but Kefauver was not invited—not until he picked up the phone and called the White House. At the signing ceremony, Richard Harris tells us, President Kennedy "wrote part of his signature, and then stopped and looked around. After a brief pause, he handed the pen to Kefauver. 'Here, you played the most important part, Estes, so you get the first pen,' he said. With an embarrassed smile, Senator Kefauver took the pen and looked at it as if he were slightly surprised. A moment later, collecting himself, he said, 'Thank you, Mr. President.' "

Kefauver had triumphed with a drug-reform bill that the New York *Times* called "monumental" because he and his staff, in the words of *The New Republic,* "knew more about the drug industry than the industry knew about itself." What is perhaps equally remarkable is that in his anxiety to win he did not still his criticisms of other New Frontier maneuvers in the hope of winning Presidential support for the drug bill.

In the hot summer of 1962, at the very climax of the drug battle, Kefauver joined with Wayne Morse and a small group of their fellow Senate liberals to oppose the administration's communications satellite bill (Comsat, for short). Kefauver found himself on the same side as Harry Truman, who said bluntly, "The damned Republicans and some Democrats are trying to give away public property."

To others it was not so cut and dried, but to Kefauver and the bloc of ten determined Senators whom he led in a filibuster, the measure was basically a giveaway of public resources (the development of rocketry had already cost the American people $20 billion) to the largest private monopoly in the world, the American Telephone and Telegraph Company. The bill, about which no one—including the administration itself—seemed to know very much, was designed to create "a private, profit-making corporation with a monopoly in the U.S. use of space for international communications." (The description is that of H. L. Nieburg, in his book *In the Name of Science*.)

Kefauver and his colleagues felt that the people who would be paying had been ill-informed, and that the only way to inform them properly would be to use the Senate floor to mount an educational program. It was not a course designed to dispose the President to aid Kefauver with the drug bill. "Nothing stood in AT&T's path," writes Joseph C. Goulden, in *Monopoly,* a study of AT&T, "but the ten Senators who hoped, by filibustering, to delay action on the legislation until after the fall elections."

Benjamin Gordon, chief staff economist for the Senate

Small Business Committee, is—like John Blair—a long-time public servant with a dedication to the public weal. He recalls how, dissatisfied with the administration's satellite bill, he had prepared, at the request of Senator Russell Long, a substitute bill which would involve the setting up of a company on the lines of TVA or the Panama Canal Company. But Long was too busy in a re-election campaign and gave him the go-ahead to "do a little propaganda and education activity and get another Senator to introduce the bill."

Gordon discussed with Bernard Fensterwald of the Kefauver staff the possibility of interesting Kefauver in the substitute bill. "While we were talking Senator Kefauver walked in. I explained it to him for two minutes, after which he said decisively, 'I'll do it.' Just like that. After that I was involved with his activity throughout the hearings on the satellite program and the filibuster."

Kefauver, writes Goulden,

stumbled across interesting intelligence concerning [Assistant Secretary of the Air Force Brockway McMillan, who had been with Bell Laboratories, an AT&T subsidiary, for fifteen years before going to the Pentagon] during a survey of former Bell people working on space communications for the government. To ascertain just what Dr. McMillan did in his Defense Department job, Kefauver obtained from the Air Force a stack of documents written by him.

"What did I find?" Kefauver asked the Senate. "Much to my amazement, I found that Dr. McMillan not only did not disqualify himself from decisions bearing on AT&T, he has also deliberately and gratuitously gone out of his way to help AT&T with the low-orbit Telstar system and disparage the efforts of AT&T's competitors who want to develop a synchronous system.

"Before that, when he was still with Bell Laboratories, he had testified and filed a statement with the FCC, in which he, with other AT&T employees, discussed the space problems in which AT&T is interested.

"I do not know to what extent Dr. McMillan has acted out of pure motives or bad motives. I do not know if he consciously intended to help AT&T. . . . I do know, however, that with his background it is shocking to find him taking on an active role in furthering the fortunes of AT&T and spiking those of its competitors, and in disparaging the Advent program, the synchronous satellite proposal."

The documents Kefauver obtained were classified secret, but he gave the gist of them to the Senate. In one paper, Kefauver said, Dr. McMillan downgraded the Syncom, "the obvious purpose of which was to . . . get us committed to the low orbit system, Telstar, or something like it."

In another document, Kefauver said, Dr. McMillan recommended that the Air Force juggle its budget to put $1,350,000 into Telstar. He spoke indignantly of the "Society of the Friends of AT&T in Government":

"I think it is obvious that the primary purpose for AT&T's honeycombing the government is to protect its monopoly and, further, to protect its huge investment in such things as underseas cables from being obsoleted by such revolutionary things as space satellites."

This time, however, there were no thalidomide babies to arouse the public to demand that its interests be protected.

Kefauver and his small band were outflanked and out-maneuvered by the public relations men and the defenders of the corporate interests. After fourteen days, the Senate leadership moved for cloture to shut off the debate.

According to Goulden,

> Only three months earlier the Senate had refused to stop a filibuster on an Administration civil rights bill aimed at ending discriminatory literacy tests for voter registration. This time the Senate imposed cloture by 63 to 27—the first time a filibuster had been voted to an end since 1927. Five embarrassed Southern Senators who supported the administration took fishing trips to avoid having to vote against a filibuster; others voted "no" only after success of cloture was assured. . . . After that the rout was swift, and AT&T lobbyists sitting in the gallery began to relax and smile expansively. . . . Did the American public and American press realize what Congress did with the Communications Satellite Act? Apparently not. . . .

For Goulden the meaning was clear: "The American Telephone & Telegraph Company persuaded Congress to bequeath it working control of America's communications satellites."

For Kefauver the meaning was painfully clear too. It was only rubbed in when President Kennedy appointed two drug-industry spokesmen to the board of Comsat—John T. Connor, head of Merck (one of the most responsible drug companies, to be sure), and Lloyd N. Cutler, special counsel to the Pharmaceutical Manufacturers Association.

Kefauver had won his drug-bill victory, but at the cost of physical exhaustion. He had lost the fight against Comsat, at the cost of more exhaustion, but he was not about to quit.

From here on out, he had to whip his own weariness, to force himself to do battle. In June 1963, he introduced a bill to establish an Office of Consumers. He wrote in, *In a Few Hands,*

> During my service in the Congress . . . I have frequently been struck by the plethora of statistical data accessible to the economic and social investigator. . . . The amazing fact is that, with all the whirl of the printing presses in this country, there are vast and important gaps in information. Time and again it has been my experience as chairman of an investigating committee in the House or Senate to find that crucial economic facts of vital consequence to the whole economy were shrouded in mystery.

Despite reversals, despite the fact that there was no immediate prospect for passage of the Office of Consumers bill, he kept returning to his basic faith in the people: "It is difficult to believe that this country will, for long, tolerate an industrial organization in which control over basic economic policy is lodged in the hands of officials of a few private corporations. Our traditions of a free, democratic society are too deep-rooted, the strain of Populist philosophy, too widely disseminated; the values involved, too great."

So when in 1963 a trade war began, which was obstructing the distribution of low-priced U.S. drugs in Latin America, he opened the fight for a new Congressional inquiry. And when Comsat reared its head again, this time asking for a $45-million appropriation of public money for a purely private-enterprise corporation, he rose once again to fight against this use of Federal treasury funds for what had originally been sold to the public as a private corporation.

Late in July, around his sixtieth birthday, Mrs. Martha Ragland stopped in to see Estes Kefauver. Tired herself from the years of battling in Tennessee for good causes, all too often to little effect, she said to him, "Estes, I really don't know how you stand it up here in Washington, where you have to see all the good things being eroded."

And he replied, "You know . . . I just about *can't* stand it any more."

The mood was familiar to Jowanda Shelton, who usually drove him back and forth to committee sessions. One night, more with weariness and resignation than with bitterness, he leaned back heavily in the car and said to her, "What's the use of my even staying on the committee? It's stacked against me."

Yet when the bell rang, neither his courage nor his sense of humor failed him. Mrs. Richard Borwick was along when he went horseback riding with several of his children, loaded down with all of the equipment that he loved to buy. As he dismounted his massive bulk, he observed that his horse was in a lather. Grinning his sad grin, he patted the sweating animal and remarked, "Okay, old buddy. Next time *I'll* carry *you.*"

There was not to be a next time. Not long after, he arose at the end of a grueling day to deliver the opening speech condemning the giveaway of public funds to Comsat. Suddenly he felt a massive blow to the heart. But he would not quit.

"When the attack struck," wrote his young committee counsel, Victor Ferrall, Jr., "Kefauver paused and in a whispered aside asked a colleague to suggest the absence of a quorum, not asking for it himself so as to avoid losing the floor. When the quorum call was terminated and debate resumed, Kefauver, still in obvious discomfort, finished his speech."

Thirty-six hours later, on August 10, 1963, Estes Kefauver was dead—some say of a ruptured artery, others of a broken heart.

an afterword ☆ Was It All Worth It?

☆☆☆ In death, Estes Kefauver's destiny was as ironic as it had been in life. That he died broke, when with a nod of the head he might—like Lyndon B. Johnson—have amassed a fortune while in public office, was not unexpected. Nor was it surprising that most of his shocked staff could not afford the fare to Madisonville, where he was to be buried on the family farm. But Kefauver himself would have been pleased that his admirer, Ward King, although a Republican capitalist, promptly came through with his own plane and flight crew when Charles Caldwell told him that twenty kids from the office couldn't get to Madisonville.

At the funeral, by all accounts a ghastly affair, the minister bore down heavily on spiritual matters but never so much as mentioned Estes Kefauver's years of public service. And the drizzle which had been weighing down on everyone along with the minister's remarks, suddenly became a torrent as those who had made the long trek from all parts of the United States gathered at the little family graveyard behind the house. Ruth Golden, publisher of the Chattanooga *Times,* cannot erase from her mind the memory of the heavens opening up in a blinding downpour just as Estes

Kefauver's coffin was being lowered into the ground.

Meanwhile, back in Washington, politicians of all shades were polishing up their oratory for the memorial addresses they would be delivering in both houses of Congress. Some of their statements are worthy of respect to this day; others form a part of what Paul Douglas has called "the repulsive spectacle" of fawning remarks, nauseating in their insincerity, by men who had sabotaged and harassed Estes Kefauver every painful step of the way.

Was this what it all came down to—some plain people and some devoted assistants weeping in the rain with family and friends, and some pompous politicos looking back with hypocritical unctuousness on his years of unrelenting struggle against them and their Big Business paymasters? Would he have achieved any more if, at the very beginning, he had chosen, like Norman Thomas or A. J. Muste, to work from outside the two-party system?

"I often wondered," Hubert Humphrey said, "from what deep source he drew the strength to carry on."

If these pages have demonstrated anything, it is that Estes Kefauver drew strength from two sources, each rare in politicians as ambitious as he, and almost never found in combination. First was his unshakable Populist faith *in* the people as against the powerful few, coupled with his adherence to the code of the landed gentry, that one chosen *by* the people has a never-ending obligation to work *for* the people—and to do so with honor, courteousness, and chivalry. Second was a profound integrity, which would never permit his conscience to do the popular thing simply because it was popular. "Estes," a West Tennessee political figure once asked, "won't you have to back up a little on the race problem?" To which Kefauver replied: "Yes—if I give up everything I believe in."

That is why Estes Kefauver could never have become an insider in the sense of joining the Senate club, or signing up in the establishment, even if that might have smoothed his path to the power and glory of the White House. It is also why this consummate vote-getter who plodded "up and down the American folkways," as Russell Baker wrote, "with his huge right hand dangling limp before him, ready for deposit in the claw of anyone who crossed his path," could not have been an ideological outsider like his courageous contemporaries Thomas or Muste, and refused to play the bourgeois political game lest it sully those big dangling hands.

The last irony of all is that the very qualities that made him an impossible candidate in the 1950's might very well have made him an unbeatable candidate in the 1970's. He opposed imperialism, as much when it was practiced by Americans as when it was imposed by Europeans or Russians. He opposed unchecked power, as much when it was abused by the clubmen in Washington as when it was abused by the tycoons of private industry. He opposed the greedy despoliation of the world in which we have to live, particularly when it attempted by stealth to undermine such beautiful achievements as that of the original TVA. And he fought with incredible energy for the poor and the friendless —black and white, working people and little businessmen, students struggling with loyalty oaths and immigrants victimized by McCarthyism.

Had he never won—not the Presidency, not any of his countless individual forays—he would still be worthy of honor for the example he set of never quitting despite the odds. But we have the testimony of independent yet committed observers, men of untrammeled spirit, as to his actual achievement.

John Blair, who knew both men very well, regards Kefauver and the radical social scientist, C. Wright Mills, an authentic hero of young Americans for the last ten years, as his two best friends. In Blair's opinion, Kefauver should be as much a model for youth as Mills (whose early work on small business had a profound effect on Kefauver). Just as our ideas about the structure and destiny of America would not be quite the same had Mills not lived, so, says Blair, "Our laws, and the practice, conduct, and structure of industry today would be quite different had Estes Kefauver not lived." The two most important pieces of anti-trust legislation since 1914, Blair points out, bear his name: the Kefauver-Celler Act of 1950 and the Kefauver-Harris Act of 1962. Of them, and their author, I. F. Stone has written: "Nobody ever achieved more against greater odds."

Indeed, no one has summed up the man better than did Stone when he hailed Kefauver as "a tribune of the people, wielding a one-man veto made possible by his integrity, industry, and courage."

Every man—even one confined to prison or to infirmity—makes his own choice as to what he will do with his life. Estes Kefauver might have chosen not to shake all those hands, but to follow what might have appeared his natural beat—aloofness, close study of our society, prescriptions as to its improvement or radical replacement. In that case the voice of the tribune would not have been heard in the halls of Congress, and the quality of our lives would be poorer than it is today.

On the other hand, he might have chosen to shake just a few more hands, and indicate his willingness to yield up his principles in exchange for the ultimate glory. In that case, even assuming the improbable—that is, his gaining the Presidency in the Age of Eisenhower—he would have been only one more Chief Executive who, in coupling a cold-blooded concern for his "image" with a slavish respect for the rich and powerful, helped turn young people away from the prospect of changing America by changing its political course.

By virtue of the choices he himself did make, Estes Kefauver tried to offer others a genuine choice. He wore himself out, yes; he accomplished only a fraction of what he had hoped to, yes. But unquestionably, could he speak today, he would say to young Americans: "As long as you understand what I was trying to do, it was all worth it."

Selected Bibliography

Anderson, Jack, and Fred Blumenthal. *The Kefauver Story.* New York: The Dial Press, 1956.

Clark, Joseph S. *Congress: The Sapless Branch.* New York: Harper & Row, 1964.

————. *The Senate Establishment.* New York: Hill & Wang, 1963.

Gorman, Joseph Bruce. *Kefauver, A Political Biography.* New York: Oxford University Press, 1971.

Goulden, Joseph C. *Monopoly.* New York: Putnam's, 1968.

Harris, Richard. *The Real Voice.* New York: Macmillan, 1964.

Herling, John. *The Great Price Conspiracy.* Washington: Robert B. Luce, Inc., 1962.

Kefauver, Estes. *Crime in America.* Edited & with an introduction by Sidney Shalett. New York: Greenwood Press, 1951.

————, with the assistance of Irene Till. *In a Few Hands.* New York: Pantheon, 1965.

————, and Dr. Jack Levin. *A Twentieth-Century Congress.* New York: Essential Books, Duell, Sloan & Pearce, 1947.

Matthews, Donald R. *U.S. Senators and Their World.* Chapel Hill: University of North Carolina Press, 1960.

Mintz, Morton. *The Therapeutic Nightmare.* Boston: Houghton Mifflin Co., 1965.

Stone, I. F. *In a Time of Torment.* New York: Vintage, 1968.

————. *The Haunted Fifties.* New York: Random House, 1963.

Streit, Clarence K. *Union Now.* New York: Harper & Bros., 1939.

Index